Spirit Filled Marriage

Spirit Filled Marriage - Bryce and Tracy Johnson

Copyright 2023©. All rights reserved.

No portion of this book may be reproduced, stored in a retrievable system, or transmitted in any form or by any means- electronic, mechanical, photocopy, recording, scanning without permission of the authors.

Scripture quotations are all taken from The Passion Translation (tPt) Passion and Fire Ministries Inc.

Published by Johnson Business Solutions LLC and lead by Holy Spirit ☺

Printed in the USA through Kindle Direct Publishing

ISBN: 9798374922998

"Heaven is on your side! As a wife or husband, you need God's supernatural grace to enjoy a supernatural marriage. Bryce and Tracy Johnson have given us such a beautiful understanding of how we all can experience a *Spirit Filled Marriage*. It is full of insights and fascinating keys to unlock hearts to a deeper commitment and a more glorious union. This book is what you've been looking for! Read it together and go through it with an open heart and it absolutely will bring you into the overflow of God's plan for your marriage! You won't be the same after reading this book!"

Dr Brian Simmons
Passion & Fire Ministries

"Spirit Filled Marriage"

"Hosting the loving care and wisdom of Holy Spirit in your marriage."

Introduction

Welcome to "Spirit Filled Marriage" and congratulations on taking meaningful steps to invest in your marriage. Thank you for your desire for more of what God has planned for you and your spouse. You are about to experience a rewarding journey with each other, AND with The One that created you. Like most things in life, this experience will be as good as the effort you put into it. Experience the material, encourage each other and follow the process. The power of this will truly be experienced and facilitated through your time with each other and Holy Spirit. He will teach you and remind you of everything (John 14:26) and will be in your conversation throughout the book as a helper and friend. No matter where you are in your marriage, whether you were married last week or many years ago, you brought your own set of expectations of what marriage would be. Many of your expectations for marriage were established and modeled through your own individual experiences. Those examples, good and bad, can get in the way of you experiencing the fullness of what God has planned for your life and for your marriage. Spirit Filled Marriage will bring you together with Holy Spirit, your spouse and possibly the unique connection with a small group walking through this journey with you. It is up to you to determine the best way to utilize this material, either one on one, in a small group or over a long weekend with other eager couples.

We have experienced the joys of celebrating renewed, refreshed and healthy marriages over many years and want to share the following simple thoughts and ideas below. These suggestions and reminders will help you experience the greatest benefit from your investment of time in this study.

*Be honest with yourself and your spouse. Be as transparent as you can throughout the process. This kind of intimacy happens through trust and openness with each other and is experienced uniquely in each person at different times. Please be thoughtful and provide room for Holy Spirit to guide you, your spouse and the others that may be in your group, in His time.

*Be self-focused and recognize it's about you and the change that will occur in you. This isn't about your spouse; this is about you and your relationship with Christ. Work on yourself and watch what God does in your life AND in the life of your spouse. This can be the most significant outcome of the process! What you experience individually will be different from others, so remember that this is a process. Take it one step at a time, one chapter at a time. Each lesson builds on the last one, so appreciate the importance of each lesson and how each one fits together throughout your experience.

*Be thoughtful and thorough with your own work. Be intentional with your prayers, in answering the questions provided in the chapter and the discussion you will have with your spouse and small group. The more you put into the process the more you will receive. We have witnessed great success over the years because of the diligent effort from those participating. Trust Holy Spirit to lead you and provide the wisdom needed for a successful experience. We're always pleased to hear "this is the best investment we have ever made in our marriage". This kind of response and experience happens through asking for His help, listening and submitting to His leadership and guidance.

*We are pleased to share all biblical references through The Passion Translation, a meaningful and fresh delivery of God's word for all of us to appreciate and enjoy.

We understand that everyone comes into this study from different backgrounds, different experiences and a different point of view. The understanding of our differences, as well as the way we complement one another will make this all the more significant. Allow Holy Spirit to guide you as your helper throughout the reading, the questions and your conversations.

Thank you for joining in the experience of Spirit Filled Marriage. As you have questions or additional needs, please reach us at

info@spiritfilledmarriage.org

Chapters

SPIRIT FILLED LOVE

Chapter 1: Love from the Father You, uniquely made: Psalm 139:13-14, 1 Corinthians 12:4-11, Proverbs 3:5, 1 Corinthians 12:12-27, 1 Corinthians 14:3-7, Romans 5:8, 1 John 4:7-21

Kingdom thinking: *God made you for relationship and intimacy with Him. Love, defined biblically by God, is out of reach without inviting Him into our life. Asking Holy Spirit to guide and lead you, to love like Him, will bring a closer relationship with Him and that of your spouse.*

Chapter 2: Imperfection comes together: James 4:1-3, Matthew 5:3, John 15:5, Psalm 139:23-24, Psalm 51:

Kingdom thinking: *Two imperfect people can come together to fulfill the Oneness that only comes from God.*

SPIRIT FILLED GRACE

Chapter 3: Spirit filled grace: Ephesians 2:4-5, Ephesians 2:8, Titus 3:3-5

Kingdom thinking: *Unmerited favor, undeserved love from the Father. You don't have to earn this, you receive it freely.*

Chapter 4: Humility: Philippians 2:1-18, Mark 10:42-45, Matthew 10:39

Kingdom thinking: *Thinking of yourself less. Having self-awareness, recognizing who you really are and how you relate to others.*

SPIRIT FILLED WORDS

Chapter 5: Communication: James 1:19, Romans 12:18, Proverbs 29:11, Matthew 5:22, 1 Corinthians 13:7, Ephesians 4:15, Proverbs 31:26

Kingdom thinking: *Communication is a powerful aspect of any relationship. Mutual understanding is how we show respect and appreciation for one another.*

Chapter 6: Communication in action: Matthew 7:5, Proverbs 19:11, Ephesians 4:2-3

Kingdom thinking: *Conflict provides opportunity for honest and intimate sharing. Conflict can lead to connection.*

SPIRIT FILLED FORGIVENESS

Chapter 7: Forgiveness: Matthew 18:15, 21-35, Proverbs 19:11, Ephesians 4:32

Kingdom thinking: *You will benefit the most from offering forgiveness. Experience the forgiveness and freedom that Jesus Christ provided you, through His life and resurrection.*

Chapter 8: Activating Forgiveness: Colossians 3:13, Psalm 139:23-24, 1 John 1:9, Psalm 51:4

Kingdom thinking: *Because of the perfect sacrifice of Jesus Christ, we can share in His example of offering forgiveness with our spouse. Marriage can be a life-long experience in learning how to forgive.*

SPIRIT FILLED TRUTH

Chapter 9: Commitment: Romans 5:10, Malachi 2:14, Mark 10:1-12

Kingdom thinking: *Understanding the meaning of Contract vs. Covenant will change your relationship with your spouse and with others.*

Chapter 10: Truth: Romans 12:2, 1 Corinthians 13:4-7, Matthew 19:6, 1 Corinthians7:28, Psalm16:11, Psalm103:10, Matthew 4:1-11, Deuteronomy 14:2

Kingdom thinking: *Worldly views of marriage may distract from biblical truth. You and your marriage have been set apart for His glory.*

SPIRIT FILLED WISDOM

Chapter 11: Expectations: Proverbs 13:12, Psalm 62:2, Philippians 4:8, Proverbs 22:3, 1 Corinthians 13:7, Psalm 73:25

Kingdom thinking: *Thinking of others and recognizing each of you have expectations, may be instrumental for your own personal growth and for your marriage.*

Chapter 12: Mutual Respect: Psalm 139:13-14, Ecclesiastes 4:9-12, Genesis 1:27-28, 1 Peter3: 7, Philippians 2:3-4, Genesis 2:24, Ephesians 5:33

Kingdom thinking: *We have been wonderfully made. We are different from one another. God will guide and assist you in holiness within your marriage.*

SPIRIT FILLED INTIMACY

Chapter 13: Intimacy: Genesis 2:24-25, Romans 5: 8, Psalm 103:10-11

Kingdom thinking: *Being fully known without fear of judgement. Knowing your spouse like Adam and Eve before the fall.*

Chapter 14: Physical intimacy: Galatians 5:1, Genesis 1:27-28, 31, 1 Corinthians 10:31, Matthew 5:28, 1 Corinthians 13: 5, Philippians 2:3-4, Romans 14:15, 1 Corinthians 7:3-5

Kingdom thinking: *Oneness is the goal of a Kingdom Marriage. It is a gift from God, equipping us for Spiritual growth and maturity.*

SPIRIT FILLED ONENESS

Chapter 15: Oneness: Genesis 2:18, Ephesians 5:25-28, Romans 8:29, 1 Thessalonians 5:14, Hebrews 10:24, 1 Thessalonians 4:10, John 5:15, James 4:1-3, Hebrews 10:25, 2 Corinthians 1:3-4, Matthew 6:19-21, Proverbs 22:6, Mark 10:45, 1 Corinthians 7:28, 1 John 13:34-35

Kingdom thinking: *The marriage covenant provides great opportunity to be intimate with your spouse. You are partnering with your spouse in spiritual oneness throughout your lives.*

The Inclusion of Holy Spirit in your Marriage

As you begin your "Spirit Filled Marriage" journey, be mindful and intentional about your investment of time and involvement with Holy Spirit. Ask Him to lead you and open your mind, body and spirit to what He has for you, throughout the process. Take time to listen and sense what He is sharing with you. How is He preparing you? How is He equipping you? Allowing His leading will produce a more intimate experience with Him and with your spouse throughout the study. Do your homework early and be sure to set aside time to discuss with your spouse. Prepare to share your thoughts and be open about what you're sensing with each other. Sharing your answers to the questions with your spouse will open unique and meaningful conversation. Prepare for and EXPECT something special to happen during your time in the study, your time discussing with your spouse and your time sharing with your small group.

The content in "Spirit Filled Marriage" is meant to work together with Holy Spirit, recognizing the powerful words found in the book of John.

John 14:16-17 *"And I will ask the Father and he will give you another Savior, the Holy Spirit of Truth, who will be to you a friend just like me and he will never leave you. The world won't receive him because they can't see him or know him. But you know him intimately because he remains with you and will live inside you"*

John 14:25-26 *"I am telling you this while I am still with you. But when the Father sends the Spirit of Holiness, the One like me who sets you free, he will teach you all things in my name. And he will inspire you to remember every word that I've told you."*

Our ability to engage the power of Holy Spirit as a significant member of The Trinity, will lead to a deeper understanding of who HE is in our lives AND in our marriage.

To facilitate this process please consider purposeful prayer each day, asking Him questions and listening for His response. He is always with you and is always interested in having a conversation with you. You might reserve some time in the quiet of the day or with one of your favorite worship songs playing in the background. However you join together with the Lord is up to you. His presence in your life and throughout this study will open doors and create opportunities that won't typically happen without Him. Recognize the significance of Holy Spirit being IN you and always with you. 1 Corinthians 6:17-20 is a great reminder of who we are in Christ, as well as who He is in our physical bodies. *We are mingled into one Spirit with Him.*

Please consider:

If you feel disconnected or that you're experiencing difficulty hearing from Holy Spirit, it could be caused from a strained relationship because of unforgiveness with your earthly mother or female caregiver. We have learned through numerous teachings and many of our own experiences that each family member contributes to the health and wellbeing of a child. We have also experienced that those who lacked a mothers care and comfort usually carry some level of "wounding" that needs to be healed. To live in connection with Holy Spirit, we need to ask for and seek healing of these past wounds.

Chapter 1: Love from The Father

"You, uniquely made"

In Genesis 1:26, the love of the Father is initiated in His creation of man. *"Let us make a man and a woman in our image to be like us"*. The reference to "US" is a powerful one, as God was there with the Son and Holy Spirit. The love of The Father is one that is significant and meaningful for every human being. His love for us began even before our conception. Because of our inability to love fully, God established His plan for us, as He has redeemed us through His son Jesus Christ. The redemptive love that He expressed for each one of us on the cross is what we recognize as His perfect model for love, in an imperfect world. We need the Triune God in our lives to understand and comprehend the depth of unconditional love that we receive and share with others.

The love that we receive from one another is a love that is shared from the experiences we've had in our own lives. It has been developed over the years from watching our parents, grandparents, friends, neighbors and many, many others that we've observed. But where does "real love" come from? Somewhere in our past we established an "expectation" of what love is supposed to look like and what it's supposed to feel like. Even as you're reading this you're thinking about your own love experiences and those that influenced your own understanding of love.

Each of us has unique and different experiences when it comes to love. Think about the love that you had growing up and what you experienced. How different was that love from others you know, specifically your spouse? The topic of love is one that has been introduced and modified in every imaginable way. It has been expressed in movies, music, television shows and every type of medium available to man since the beginning of time. The power of love can bring us together, it can be a force for change and it can overwhelm us with emotion. It can also be a force for manipulation, performance requirements and just plain struggle.

Many times it becomes one that is merit based and can be seen as a process or method to an end. One thing we know for sure is that God has a love for us that will never be matched or fully understood. Our goal is to reach a better understanding of His love and His desire for a deeper relationship with each one of us, through our relationship with our spouse.

You were wonderfully made for His purpose and for His glory. Many times we miss or forget the significance of our existence, because of our past or because of the lies we've believed. When we identify ourselves as Christians and truly recognize our identity IN CHRIST, we can be confident in "who we are" as heirs to the throne of God, His child, a part of His Royal Priesthood. If we know who and whose we are, the challenges from the evil one won't sway us from our true identity and God's calling on our lives. Romans 8:15-16 shares some beautiful words about who we are in Christ. *"You did not receive the Spirit of religious duty, leading you back into the fear of not being good enough. You have received the Spirit of full acceptance."* Take a minute to read both verses and allow Holy Spirit to love you and lead you into the FULL awareness of who you are. You are God's beloved child! Believe it and live the full life that He has for you!

Recognize HIS love for you and HIS desire to have a deep relationship with you, through His Son, Jesus Christ.

Biblical Truth:
Psalm 139:13-14 (wonderfully made), 1 Corinthians 12:4-11 (Spiritual gifts), Proverbs 3:5 (Trust in the Lord), 1 Corinthians 12:12-27 (Unity in the body, diversity) Romans 5:8 (Christ died for us), 1 John 4:7-21 (Love one another) Romans 8:15-16 (Identity)

Appreciation for how He made me

Psalm 139:14 in The Passion Translation has some real power to it and should bring confidence for all of us. *"I thank you, God, for making me so mysteriously complex! Everything you do is marvelously breathtaking. It simply amazes me to think about it! How thoroughly you know me, Lord!"* How much more confidence should we have, knowing that we have a Heavenly Father that created us for His purpose, in His image? Even more, you were created with a certain DNA and a specific role in the "body of Christ". Our Spiritual Gifts connect us to *Father God* and allow us to function in the body, each and every day. The entire chapter of 1 Corinthians 12 shares a great message of who we are in the body and how we are to function as one. Please be sure to read it now while it's fresh on your mind. As we recognize our own unique gifting and how we participate in this world with other believers, our purpose and the significance of our part in the body becomes real and meaningful. We can also be confident in the One that created us, as we learn to trust Him and His guidance in our lives. Proverbs 3:5 shares the power of our trust in Him and not to lean on or rely on our own opinions or understanding. We need to rely on Him for everything, to allow Him to lead and love us in every decision we make along the way.

Wedding Bells

Think of the last wedding you attended and hearing the reading of "the love verses" during the ceremony. As we participate as witnesses in the ceremony, seeing the couple join together in a covenant relationship, we are witnesses to the power of Paul's words and his teaching to the church in Corinth. The verses found in 1 Corinthians 13:4-7 are powerful and provide a wonderful description of love and how we are to "love one another". This is a love letter. These are the words that God has expressed to each one of us, not just during the marriage ceremony but through each day of our lives. He shares a model of love described that is much different from that of the world. This LOVE is sacrificial and selfless. It is a love that only comes from Father God.

READ: 1 Corinthians 13:4-7

Love is large and incredibly patient.

It is bigger than what we can imagine or share. It is so much bigger than what we experience in our daily lives, so let us bring heaven to earth in the form of His love for us. It doesn't look for a quick response or anything immediate, it waits and encourages thoughtfully along the way.

Love is gentle and consistently kind to all.

It represents a kindness and gentleness that only comes from the presence of The Lord. It comes from the Gifts of the Spirit that Holy Spirit shares with all of us as Christians. It is a reminder of the love of Christ and His powerful example of agape love.

It refuses to be jealous when blessing comes to someone else.

It celebrates others and lifts others up, unselfishly. It recognizes other unique gifting and the compliments that we have with each other. It acknowledges our differences and moves us to accept others in an open and honest way.

Love does not brag about one's achievements nor inflates its own importance.

There is an understanding of His presence in us and an awareness of His power through us. In our weakness He is strong. That strength can be seen in our humble response and service to others, placing others in a higher position, serving their needs before our own.

Love does not traffic in shame and disrespect, nor selfishly seek its own honor.

This love is defined by what we have in our identity in Christ. It is His love in us, not living in shame and not disrespecting others. It is about building others up and respecting one another's past and their life experience. We love others because He first loved us!

Love is not easily irritated or quick to take offense.

It can withstand a lot of the challenges and distractions of the day, without becoming resentful or upset. It is gracious and forgiving with the small offenses, which are typically offensive because of our own self needs or attitudes.

Love joyfully celebrates honesty and finds no delight in what is wrong.

As we live life, we recognize that transparency and vulnerability with others leads to healthy relationships, as we share honestly with each other. Love is full and expectant of meaningful, fruitful conversations and encouragement for others.

Love is a safe place of shelter, for it never stops believing the best for others.

It establishes a place of honesty, peace and trust for one another. It opens doors to honest, open conversations of understanding. It celebrates in an upbeat, positive way, expecting the best in others.

Love never takes failure as defeat, for it never gives up.

It recognizes and appreciates the hardships of others and empathetically joins together. It has an understanding of those challenges and stays committed, regardless of the outcome. This love never fails or complains. It believes the best and expects the best.

We love because He first loved us

As you read the verses from "biblical truth" for this chapter, you recognize the significance of God's love for each of us, *"while we were sinners, Christ died for us"* in Romans 5:8. We didn't have to be in a place of perfection or good standing. He didn't wait for us to be good enough for us to earn His love; He came even in spite of who we are and what we've done. He LOVES us! We need that kind of example of love, knowing we are ill prepared to love our spouse like we promised in our vows.

1 John 4:7 throughout the chapter, John provides a great template for how we are to love. What great instruction for all of us, in terms that we can all understand. God knew that we would be challenged with loving others, but his instruction through John gives such a powerful description of how we are to love one another. We love because He first loved us is significant. Our love for Him is foremost in the process of recognizing our inability to love. By living a life of trust WITH and IN Him, we can express the kind of love that He desires for us.

We do not have a big enough view or definition of love. None of us have the ability to love effectively without God's help, so depending upon Him is the first step to a meaningful life with Him and a successful marriage with our spouse. No matter where you are in your walk with The Lord and regardless of how you feel about your marriage, there is always room for growth. Is it your desire to have the tools and connection with your spouse, or is it reconnection or resurrection that brings you to this study? Whatever the need, this study will help you recognize your inability to love without Him, as Holy Spirit guides you to the marriage God intended for you!

Questions/Activities/Activations:

Answer question 1-4 on your own, then with your spouse, as you prepare and anticipate time with your small group. You will benefit by sharing your answers and feelings in three unique settings. There is significant power in asking Holy Spirit to guide you here too. He will guide your thoughts and emotions for a very unique experience throughout the process.

Question One: What has shaped your view of love, from childhood, school days, and adulthood? How has that affected the way you love and interact with others and specifically, your spouse?

Question Two: Think about your parents love for one another... how did they share love with you and with each other? How has that expression of love influenced your own marriage?

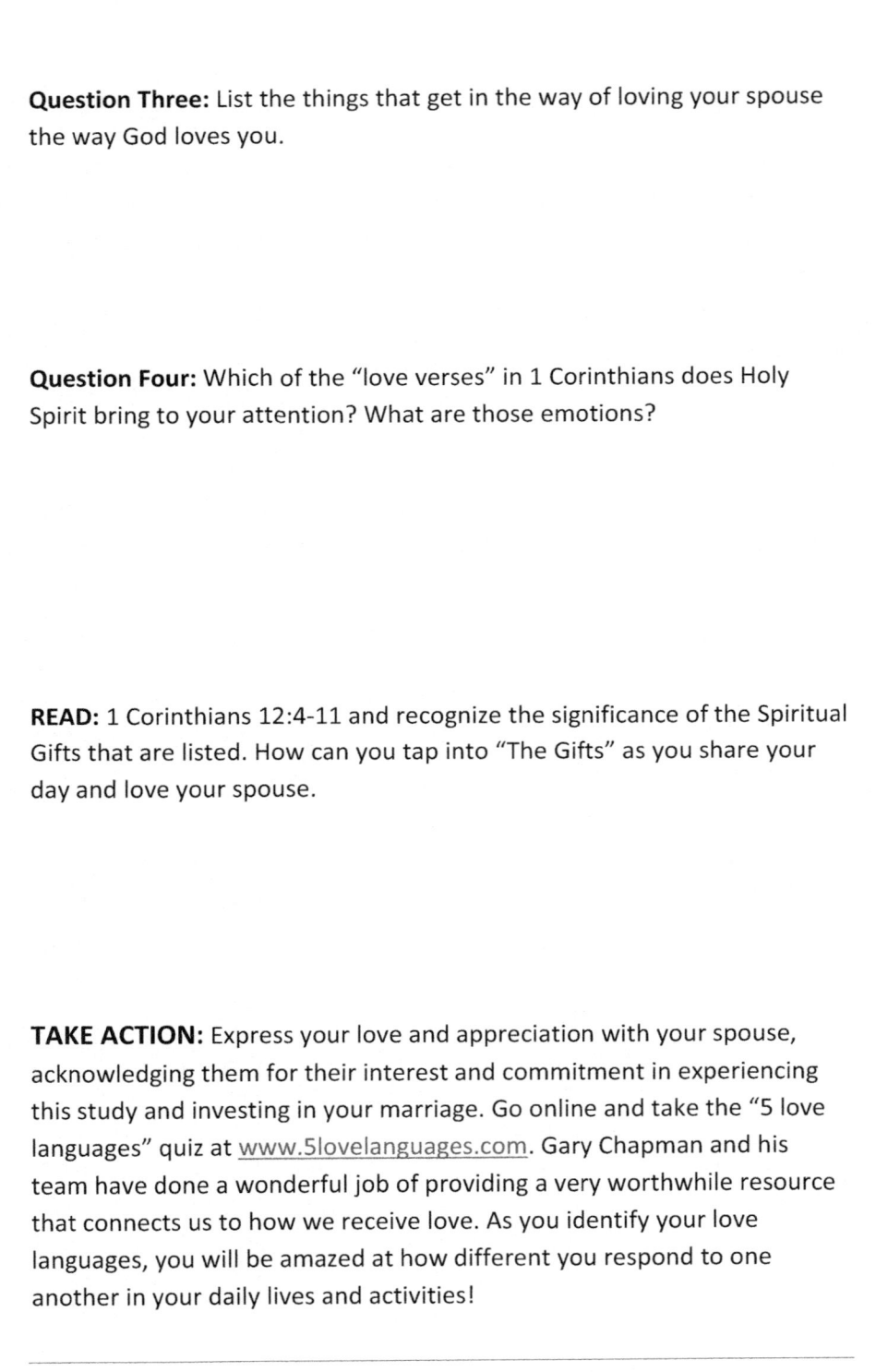

Question Three: List the things that get in the way of loving your spouse the way God loves you.

Question Four: Which of the "love verses" in 1 Corinthians does Holy Spirit bring to your attention? What are those emotions?

READ: 1 Corinthians 12:4-11 and recognize the significance of the Spiritual Gifts that are listed. How can you tap into "The Gifts" as you share your day and love your spouse.

TAKE ACTION: Express your love and appreciation with your spouse, acknowledging them for their interest and commitment in experiencing this study and investing in your marriage. Go online and take the "5 love languages" quiz at www.5lovelanguages.com. Gary Chapman and his team have done a wonderful job of providing a very worthwhile resource that connects us to how we receive love. As you identify your love languages, you will be amazed at how different you respond to one another in your daily lives and activities!

Resources and Considerations: Make use of other outside resources, like DISC assessment, Myers Briggs test or other methods for recognizing your own unique gifting and personalities. The more you know about yourself and your spouse, the more you'll appreciate the complement that you are for one another. God brought you together for His glory and to be an expression of His love for you and for others!

What are you seeing, hearing, or sensing from Holy Spirit?

Having a better understanding of His presence in your life and tapping into your own level of self-awareness will be a powerful attribute for your own spiritual growth. You may be surprised at how He wants to engage, contribute and speak to you! By asking yourself what are you seeing, hearing or sensing, you will be amazed at what He shares with you. If this is your first time with this type of experience, take it slow and open yourself to something new. You will be changed by the Helper in a way that you didn't completely understand before or even know was possible. For others this will be a rekindling of your growing relationship with Him. We look forward to you experiencing something really special in the chapters to come.

Share your thoughts here as you begin your study.

1. Holy Spirit, What Am I Seeing, Hearing or Sensing?

2. What plan do you have for me as I read this material?

3. What do you have planned for US, as we read together?

Chapter 2: Imperfection comes together

The love that we read about in the first chapter is the kind of love that we are all interested in experiencing. It is also a love that sometimes seems out of reach, doesn't it? We have our hearts set on a love that looks and sounds like what we read in chapter one, but how do two imperfect people come together to share in that kind of love?

Much of what we desire is born out of expectations from our own childhood or dreams that we have had over the years. Those expectations may be hard to meet if we don't have some guidance and direction from Our Heavenly Father. A love that comes from the Father is one that is full of the fruits of the spirit and is always consistent. How do we as two imperfect people come together to experience the GOD SIZED love that is available to us? We take time to get to know Him, study Him and learn from Him, just as we do with other relationships.

As we get to know one another in marriage, we learn to adapt and we learn to accept. What about this great marriage we dreamed about and anticipated? What changed from the days of dating and our time together before our wedding day? Two people from two different backgrounds with two different personalities have come together, living together and experiencing the challenges of daily life. No matter the amount of time you've been married, be aware of the following:

We can easily begin to make our list of things that are wrong or need to be changed. Many times **we** see those things that need to be changed in the other person.

We may see our marriage as being less than, because of comparisons we make with other marriages, or **we** recognize that things are just not meeting my ideal expectations.

We define our marriage by our circumstances, those things on the outside.

We live in a world full of many distractions.

We are misled by the world and forget about our foundation in our marriage.

James 4:1-3 asks the questions about our conflicts and quarrels that we have with each other. He addresses the question of where the battle comes from; recognizing that much of it comes from our own selfish desires. Take time to read these 3 verses in James and understand the significant meaning in your own life. As you're reading, allow Holy Spirit to share His direction for your life and the message that He has for you. Reaching out to God and allowing Holy Spirit to guide you is a great first step to a successful life, which can lead to a successful marriage.

Biblical Truth: 1 Corinthians 14:3-7 (Edifying the body), James 4:1-3 (What causes quarrels), Matthew 5:3 (The Beatitudes), John 15:5, (I am the vine) Psalm 139:23-24 (Search me oh God), Psalm 51 (David's repentance, forgiveness after sin)

Daily application:

Paul David Tripp is one of our favorite Christian authors, counselors and teachers. He provides a wonderful visual for all of us, as he suggests that we ***"draw a circle around ourselves and work on changing everyone inside the circle."*** Many times we believe the need to improve our marriage begins with the other person. It reminds me of the familiar verse in Matthew 7:5 *"You're being hypercritical and a hypocrite! First acknowledge and deal with your own 'blind spots,' and then you'll be capable of dealing with the 'blind spot' of your friend."* There is so much biblical truth around this subject we could fill many pages with the descriptions of love that come from the Father.

Even in the presence of His great love for us, our imperfections come together and get in the way of the love that God has intended for us. As He lives in each one of us, through His Son Jesus, He has a plan for sharing that love through Holy Spirit and prophetic words of encouragement through others. Prophetic words are words of encouragement to edify and build up those around us. God has a direct and powerful purpose for your life, for each one of us, as we serve in the body of Christ. We are to serve and support one another, unselfishly. Our ability to work together and serve one another is a powerful example of what He desires for us as a community of believers.

Our imperfections and selfish desires prevent us from making the connection with Our Creator and Savior, which ultimately gets in the way of us developing healthy relationships with each other. When you recognize your own brokenness and that your own hurts and personal pain contribute to how you operate in this life, then you can begin the process of healing and restoration. It may be obvious, but you are one of two people that come into your marriage. If you have been silent or avoided the conflicts and issues from your past, it will affect your relationship with your spouse and others. Coming together in a loving, compassionate way, addressing the issues in your relationship together, can lead to significant change. You may even consider some inner healing that can be done through a number of resources in your community or through your local church.

A healthy marriage consists of two people that are whole, with an understanding for each other. God sent His Son to die for you as a sacrifice for sin and for the healing of your body and mind. The good news is that you can make a difference. You can take steps to kingdom oneness as you ask Holy Spirit for His guidance and direction. The steps that you take for your own healing begin with your own self-awareness. Both are well presented in one of the most significant moments in the ministry of Jesus. They are powerful words shared by Him in The Sermon on the Mount, as He lists the Beatitudes in Matthew 5:3..."*Blessed are the poor in spirit, for theirs is the Kingdom of God.*" Acknowledging our brokenness, that we truly are poor in spirit, can open doors for us to take steps into a personal relationship with Jesus. That relationship will develop a deeper awareness of our own need and dependence on Him for everything, including a meaningful relationship with our spouse.

Now What?

Put action to these thoughts. Ask Holy Spirit for His power to help you to love, lead, forgive and take you into a deeper appreciation for what He has for both of you. John 15:5 does such a wonderful job of describing our dependence on "The Vine". *"I am the sprouting vine and you're my branches. As you live in union with me as your source, fruitfulness will stream from within you, but when you live separated from me you are powerless."* What is Holy Spirit saying to you as you read these beautiful verses in The Passion Translation? As you continue to read through the chapter, you will see the power of His life in you, the branch. Without Him you cannot live, but "connected to the vine" He will give you life and abundant fruit. How does this apply to marriage you ask? Think about the power that we can tap into, recognizing that we really are powerless to respond in a way that is "fruitful" without His strength and guidance. We are incapable of responding in a loving way when we are acting out of our own disappointment or resentment. We need the loving care of Holy Spirit to go before us, recognizing our inability to love the way He loves us.

Chapter 2 is about acknowledging and appreciating the joining of two imperfect people in a marriage. Recognize that this fact could create challenges that you didn't expect or plan for. Two different people with a life of experiences, habits, expectations, thoughts, dreams and so on, coming together to love and live a life together will take work. Calling on the power of God's presence and His plan for your lives is available to all of us.

Questions/Activities/Activations:

Answer questions 1-3 on your own, then with your spouse, as you prepare and anticipate time with your small group or other couples. You will benefit by sharing your answers and feelings in three unique settings.

Question One: Self-awareness is one thing, but asking The Lord to gaze into my heart is quite another. Read Psalm 139 and recognize the significance of David's words. Specifically look at verses 23 and 24 and allow Him to bring attention to how He knows you. List the items that come to mind to determine any path of pain that you're walking in and share them with your spouse. (Examples may include; being prideful, lazy, controlling, critical, selfish, moody...)

Question Two: After asking and hearing His words from question one, how have your actions, attitudes and sins created challenges in your relationships and in your marriage? How have they been offensive to your spouse? Share with each other and show empathy, as you listen and appreciate the honesty of each other through each item you share.

Question Three: How can you tap into The Vine, the power and His purpose for your lives together? John 15:5 says that "when you live separated from me, you are powerless". Share some ways that God can help you in your marriage, as you rely and trust in Him. Ask Him to intervene and JOIN you in your marriage, in your lives! How much more powerful will you be and how much more fruit will you bear?

READ: Read Psalm 51 and describe what you feel, sense or hear...This is your opportunity to tap into what the Lord wants to share with you, personally. Make use of this intimate time together, as He shares His love and leading for your life!

TAKE ACTION: Affirming others can be one of the most mutually rewarding things we do as we live life together. Share encouraging, affirming words with your spouse this week that will lift them up and assist them with recognizing their own unique qualities.

Chapter 3: Spirit Filled Grace

"Grace, grace…The significance of Humility…"

We open this chapter with an introduction to grace, a powerful solution to many challenges we face in life. Grace is defined as unmerited favor, it cannot be earned, it is given to you. If this is a new concept then you will appreciate its significance, especially for its meaning and contribution in a relationship. The challenges we face in life typically involve a misunderstanding or disagreement. Misunderstandings can easily move us into emotional shut down or cause us to *react* in a way that doesn't bring life to our relationships. Disagreements are usually self-focused with a lack of understanding for the others point of view. Offering GRACE in each situation can be a beautiful way of expressing love and compassion with your spouse. That kind of response requires a level of humility and selflessness that isn't always understood or recognized in our world. Ephesians 2:4-5 provides a wonderful example of God's love for each of us. *"But God still loved us with such great love. He is so rich in compassion and mercy. Even when we were dead and doomed in our many sins, he united us into the very life of Christ and saved us by his wonderful grace."* His grace was displayed and expressed for each of us, even when we didn't deserve it. Many of us may recognize the definition as unmerited favor or undeserved love. Whatever your understanding is of the term, God has poured out his grace on each of us. One of the most recognized definitions can be found in Ephesians 2 verse 8 *"For by grace you have been saved by faith. Nothing you did could ever earn his salvation, for it was the love gift from God that brought us to Christ."*

Biblical Truth: Ephesians 2:4-5 (Rich in mercy), Ephesians 2:8 (By grace...), Titus 3:3-5 (We were foolish), Colossians 4:6 (Drenched)

Daily application:

We have heard many stories about people's misunderstanding of God's love. For years, as we attended church or heard from family and friends, the message shared was that His love needed to be earned in some way. If I do this or if I do that, THEN He will love me and I will be on His good side. If I give enough, read enough, pray enough... the examples and stories are numerous, but the same powerful truth is that it comes from HIS GRACE, where His love is freely given. There is no need to earn His love. The need to *earn love* has made its way into our marriages too. The process of earning love and the response with your spouse has become merit based, one based on your performance in the marriage. There is a requirement where you must perform in a way that I think you should perform, or I won't love you. This is no way to go through any kind of meaningful relationship and certainly not a marriage.

When you have a marriage based on Grace in comparison to that of works, it becomes something special and meaningful for both of you. The understanding and application of grace in your own relationships is something to be keenly aware of. When it comes to practical use and applying this to your daily life, there is beautiful instruction for grace found in Colossians 4:6. *"Let every word you speak be drenched with grace and tempered with truth and clarity. For then you will be prepared to give a respectful answer to anyone who asks about your faith."* If you have accepted Christ as your Savior, He lives in you and therefore His kindness can be expressed through you, even in the toughest of times. We are in need of His power, so that we can love and offer grace to our spouse, just as He has done for each of us. Having the understanding that you have received HIS grace and kindness, may allow for an easier extension of His example of grace to others.

The significance of grace

Many of us have lived our lives without the true understanding of grace. What has shaped your experience with grace? How has grace been extended to you throughout your life, how was it modeled? In Titus 3:3-5 it says *"For it wasn't that long ago that we behaved foolishly in our stubborn disobedience. We were easily led astray as slaves to worldly passions and pleasures. We wasted our lives in doing evil, and with hateful jealousy we hated others. When the extraordinary compassion of God our Savior and his overpowering love suddenly appeared in person, as the brightness of a dawning day, he came to save us. Not because of any virtuous deed that we have done but only because of his extravagant mercy."* What a great reminder of whose we are and where we've been. He came to save us and renew us, even in our mess and disobedience. When you truly understand the power and significance of His love and GRACE, you may be interested or even compelled to share it with others.

Grace that may be offensive

Most people will agree wholeheartedly with the biblical references to grace. Some people may be offended and turned off when they hear someone even mention the *need* for grace. If pride is an issue, you may believe that you are good enough, loveable enough, and perfect enough that you don't need anyone's grace. Grace has now become OFFENSIVE. The truth is that NONE of us are good enough. We all need grace, especially in a marriage relationship. The real power of grace can be seen in how we respond and how we think about each other. Grace in action looks like seeing the best in each other, with a simple reminder that we are on the same team. He is not your enemy; she is not your enemy. The enemy is the enemy! The two of you need to be working together in this world, let's advocate for each other.

There can be a significant shift with this simple reminder. Think about _responding_ thoughtfully to your spouse's comments, instead of _reacting_ emotionally. Responding with grace is unselfish and thoughtful. When you respond, you're thinking of the other person as an equal, advocating for them. Grace is empathetic and understanding. As you extend grace it will be appreciated when it is extended back to you. It's reciprocal. Self-awareness and the ability to see two individuals as ONE will bring clarity to your relationship, with a focus on setting each other up for success.

BIG POINT: Offering grace does not mean that you condone the action or attitude that is expressed toward you. It can be your opportunity to introduce a selfless way to respond, in times of challenge. It is your opportunity to lead, initiate and model this biblical display of grace to your spouse. Sharing this sensitive expression to the other person, even when it's difficult, can be a game changer and powerful relationship builder for years to come.

WHAT are you seeing, hearing or sensing at this point? God is opening your senses to the message that He has for you. Take some time and ask Holy Spirit how you are to respond. What are you supposed to be learning from the definitions of grace? Remember that you have been brought together for great purpose, to complement one another and serve together. Recognize the biblical truth found in Ecclesiastes 4:9 where "two are better than one". Share below.

Here is a great exercise of grace in action.

Grace LOOKS like:

Not focusing on your spouse's faults

Choosing to believe the best about your spouse's words and actions

Not being shocked or angry when your spouse's actions aren't perfect

Not bringing up the ways your spouse has disappointed or hurt you in the past

Responding kindly to harsh words or a cold shoulder

Being an advocate for your spouse rather than building a case against them

Loving your spouse not because of their actions, but in spite of them

Questions/Activities/Activations:

Answer question 1-4 on your own, then with your spouse, as you prepare and anticipate time with your small group. Remember, you will benefit by sharing your answers and feelings in three unique settings, so be intentional in your thoughts and allow Holy Spirit to guide you in the process.

Question One: How have you experienced grace in your life AND what have you learned through this chapter. List some responses of how you're feeling and why.

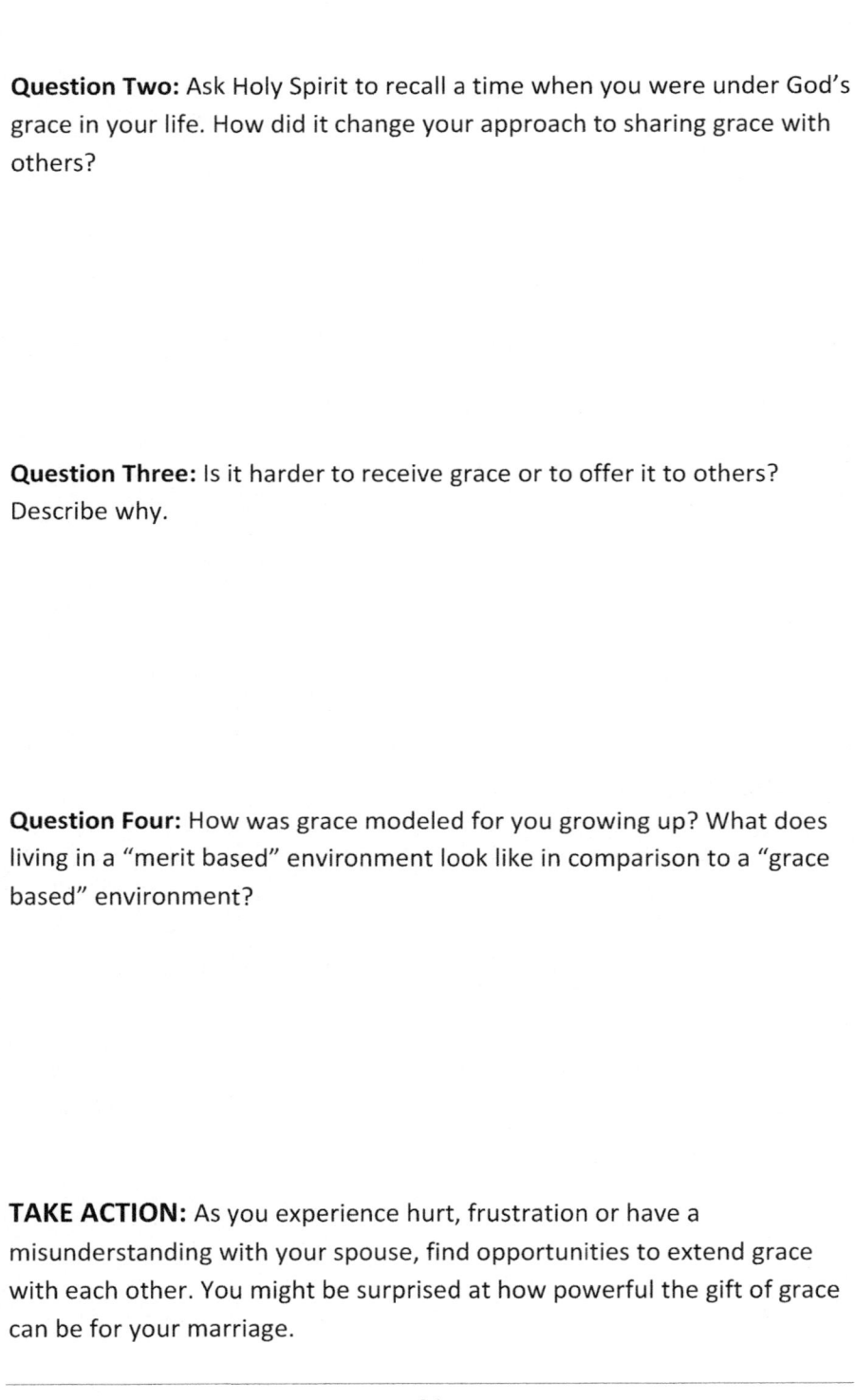

Question Two: Ask Holy Spirit to recall a time when you were under God's grace in your life. How did it change your approach to sharing grace with others?

Question Three: Is it harder to receive grace or to offer it to others? Describe why.

Question Four: How was grace modeled for you growing up? What does living in a "merit based" environment look like in comparison to a "grace based" environment?

TAKE ACTION: As you experience hurt, frustration or have a misunderstanding with your spouse, find opportunities to extend grace with each other. You might be surprised at how powerful the gift of grace can be for your marriage.

Chapter 4: Humility

Biblical reference to humility can be found many times throughout the bible, as seen in Proverbs 11:2 *"When you act with presumption, convinced that you're right, don't be surprised if you fall flat on your face! But humility leads to wisdom"*. Webster defines humility as "freedom from pride or arrogance". CS Lewis shared his understanding of humility as "not thinking less of yourself, but thinking of yourself less". This humble approach in recognizing who we are and how we are to respond can be a real benefit in any and all of our relationships. The recognition of and the need for humility, seems to be something that we all deal with; based on our life experience and the number of times it's referenced in the bible. Proverbs 22:4 in The Passion Translation is so powerful... *"Laying your life down in tender surrender before the Lord will bring life, prosperity, and honor as your reward."* What a verse to breathe life into our day and into relationships with each other. The "laying down" is all about our own ability to humble ourselves in the presence of our Heavenly Father, as we live our lives WITH and FOR Him. Allowing Him to lead us will produce wonderful things if we recognize our own prideful ways. We have all heard the statement, "I just need to get out of my own way". Well, stepping back and allowing God to do His work IN us can be a real catalyst for change.

Chapter 4 describes the power of humility and brings attention to our need to live a humble life, putting others before ourselves. Imagine what that looks like in a marriage. As we read in Philippians 2:3 *"Be free from pride-filled opinions, for they will only harm your cherished unity. Don't allow self-promotion to hide in your hearts, but in authentic humility put others first and view others as more important than yourselves"*. Some of the most memorable moments in life can be those where we give honor to someone else or sacrifice our own need to be seen, in place of someone else's need for recognition. Can you think of a time where you stepped into a place of humility? Ask Holy Spirit to bring to mind a time where you allowed someone else to shine. Remembering the emotion you experienced can be powerful. It could be a time where you honored someone receiving an award or maybe a time you stood up at a wedding, waiting for the bride to walk down the aisle. How does a groom feel as he stands at the front of the church, watching his bride walk down the aisle with everyone recognizing her as the center of attention? Think about those moments and appreciate the feelings of humility that take place in your own heart and mind. Recognizing that I'm not the most important person in the room is a simple form of humility.

Biblical Truth: Proverbs 11:2, 16:18, 22:4, Philippians 2:1-18, 2:3, Mark 10:42-45, Colossians 3:12-14

Daily application:

Your view from a place of humility:

What does humility look like in your own life and how does it look in your marriage? This can be a surprise for many, as you think of yourself less and appreciate the spouse that has been given to you to complement your life. The ideas shared below are not an exhaustive list, but are certainly good to understand and implement in your own marriage.

Thinking the best of your spouse: This is a great first step in just about everything we do, especially when it comes to communication and sharing. Thinking the best of your spouse will START any thought process or interaction with optimism.

Serve your spouse well: Put the other person first. We all have chores and tasks that we do each day. Think about a way to serve your spouse in a thoughtful way that doesn't require any kind of expected return. This is a great way to show that you care, appreciate and recognize them. Letting your spouse feel SEEN and understood is a wonderful way to place them forward and feel loved.

Knowing your spouse: You can express humility by recognizing your spouse's likes and dislikes. What makes them smile, what do they enjoy doing? What makes them feel loved? It will take an investment of time and effort, but as you determine their likes and dislikes you are showing them that you're interested in serving and supporting their interests and needs.

Speaking kindly to your spouse: Even when your spouse is having a bad day or is unkind at some point during a conversation or event, responding kindly, without raising your voice or overreacting can be a powerful expression of humility.

Recognizing your spouse: You are not competing with your spouse; you are on the same team. Show appreciation and celebrate your spouse's achievements and accomplishments. Set them up for success and you will be celebrated too.

Sharing grace: Many times we get caught in a simple debate or we argue about establishing the facts of a particular event. Choosing not to correct your spouse and admitting your wrong, can be a great way to express humility. Life together is a shared experience, full of understanding.

Admit when you're wrong: There will be times when you hurt or disappoint your spouse. Acknowledging, accepting responsibility and showing empathy for your spouse is a great way to express humility.

Make your spouse feel heard and recognized: Repeat what the other person said. "So what I heard you say," will help them feel understood and cared for. Active listening with all of your senses is an open door to good reciprocal communication.

Putting the needs of your spouse first: Understand that your needs are different. Humility looks like recognizing this simple fact and placing the needs of your spouse above your own. Put forth the goal of setting each other up for success and work as a team.

One of the most powerful examples and expressions of humility was the life of Jesus. He came to serve as an example for all of us, even from the humble beginnings in a manger. The Gospel of Mark shares the story of "The 12" concerned about who was the greatest. Mark 10:43-45 *"You are to lead by a different model. If you want to be the greatest, then live as one called to serve others. The path to promotion comes by having the heart of a bond-slave who serves everyone. For even the Son of Man did not come expecting to be served by everyone, but to serve everyone, and to give his life as the ransom price for the salvation of many."* Our society is counter of being humble, as we compete for space, position and power. Social media continues to inflate the egos of many, in a way of "likes and clicks", but the example of Jesus's life as a servant leader is counter to what we experience each day. Humility in our service to one another in our busy lives may go unnoticed and could be risky to some. Jesus is asking us to join Him in that experience of humility, just as He did in His life. Our culture is so counter to the biblical teachings of Christ; sometimes it's tough to know what's right and what's wrong. When you truly understand the grace that has been given to you and the sacrifice that has been made for your sin, the humility will come.

The other side of Humility

This may be an obvious statement, but PRIDE needs to be recognized and reckoned with here. Pride runs hand in hand with fear and control too, so be aware of your feelings and recognize the way pride sneaks into your life. Proverbs 16:18 provides a powerful reminder for all of us. *"Your boast becomes a prophecy of a future failure. The higher you lift yourself up in pride, the harder you'll fall in disgrace"*. Be aware of your pride, ask Holy Spirit to help eliminate your pride and He will lead you to enjoy a life of humility. Thinking of yourself less and putting others first, including your spouse, will open even more doors of successful relationships that pride never will.

Questions/Activities/Activations:

Answer questions 1-4 on your own, then with your spouse, as you prepare and anticipate time with your small group. Remember, you will benefit by sharing your answers and feelings in three unique settings, so be intentional in your thoughts and allow Holy Spirit to guide you in the process.

Question One: As you think of being humble and showing humility, what does that look like in your daily life with your spouse and with others?

Question Two: How do you OR how can you show humility with your spouse? Ask Holy Spirit for His guidance here too.

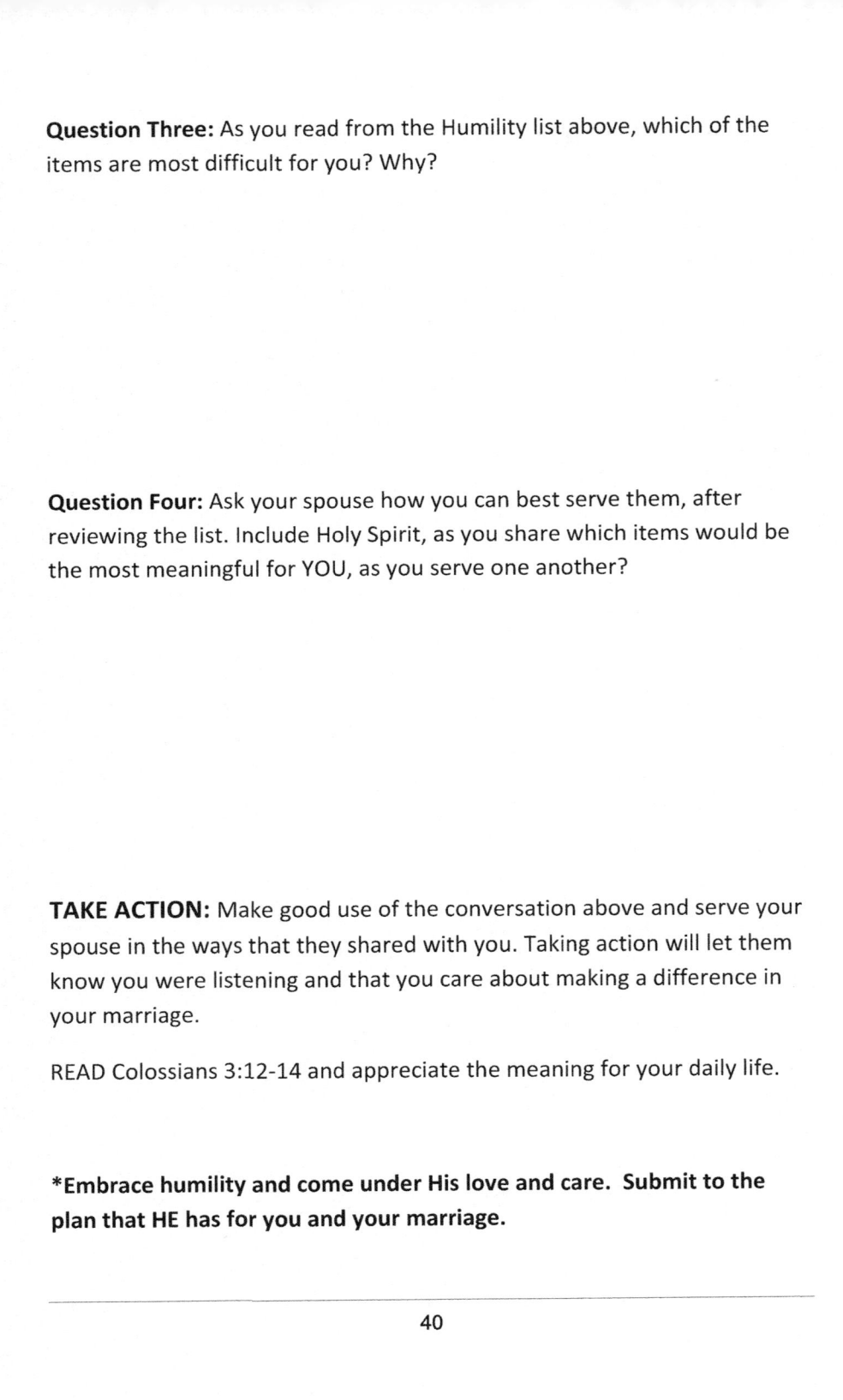

Question Three: As you read from the Humility list above, which of the items are most difficult for you? Why?

Question Four: Ask your spouse how you can best serve them, after reviewing the list. Include Holy Spirit, as you share which items would be the most meaningful for YOU, as you serve one another?

TAKE ACTION: Make good use of the conversation above and serve your spouse in the ways that they shared with you. Taking action will let them know you were listening and that you care about making a difference in your marriage.

READ Colossians 3:12-14 and appreciate the meaning for your daily life.

***Embrace humility and come under His love and care. Submit to the plan that HE has for you and your marriage.**

Chapter 5: Communication

"How do I communicate?"

A number of years ago, Stephen Covey shared some powerful words and 7 habits in his book, "7 Habits of Highly Effective People". The book seemed to set the standard on the basics of communication. Habit number 5 is, "seek first to understand then to be understood". How can this understanding affect the way we communicate with another person? There is real power in listening, but many times we get caught up in the desire to share our own story, our point of view and our own opinion before thinking about the other person. The goal of communication is to establish mutual understanding. It's not about being heard or being right or making sure that the other person agrees with you.

James 1:19 says *"My dearest brothers and sisters, take this to heart: Be quick to listen, but slow to speak. And be slow to become angry."* Can you feel the meaning of these words from Holy Spirit through James? The intentionality that is expressed is powerful. He's stating the need for listening and understanding, before escalating with your own opinion. Mutual understanding will lead you to mutual respect and awareness for the other person that you may not fully appreciate until you are slow to speak.

*Recognize the significance of this "goal" of mutual understanding and watch your life and your relationship with your spouse intensify.

Biblical Truth: James 1:19, 4:6, Romans 12:18, 12:16, Proverbs: 18:6, 29:11, 31:26, Matthew 5:22, 1 Corinthians 3:16, 13:7, Ephesians 4:15, 1 Peter 5:5

Daily application:

We communicate each day in many types of methods and mediums. Speaking is typically our most used method of communicating, but don't forget the nonverbal communication that takes place throughout the day. Some of the most powerful ways you communicate to others, including your spouse, are not found in words at all. Think of the early days of your relationship and how conscious you were of everything you were expressing and communicating to your future spouse. You had your very best on display, as you were communicating in every available method, presenting yourself as attractive, interesting and desirable. It was like you had your own public relations firm employed to present the very best of who you are to the other person. Is that still happening today in your relationship? If not, when did that stop and why? Our need to communicate our best self with each other needs to continue, as we live life through the changes and challenges of our relationship. Communicating your love and commitment to your spouse can be in words, in actions and in the way you present yourself throughout your marriage.

Negative / Toxic Communication Patterns

Much of what we experience in our communication with each other is derived from our family, our past, our history and learned behavior. We all seem to know HOW to communicate, but our methods in doing so may not be the healthiest for having successful, meaningful relationships. If you haven't done so already, begin to create a level of awareness of who you are in your own communication style. As you do, anticipate healthy patterns and healthier relationships going forward. The following list of negative communication patterns has been adapted from a book "A Lasting Promise" by Scott Stanley, Daniel Trathen, Savanna McCain and Milt Bryan. There are multiple examples of similarly named patterns that we all experienced in our lives, but these seem to be very applicable and significant.

Withdrawal and Avoid

How do I recognize it in myself?

You feel an unwillingness to start or to stay engaged in an important discussion.

When the other person brings up an issue, you retreat so you don't have to discuss it.

You know of something that you should face and discuss, but you avoid bringing it up.

What it looks like:

You walk away or leave the room in order to end an argument.

You shut down in the middle of a conversation, or change the subject.

It may include lying or saying that you agree with your spouse, just so the argument will be over.

What to do:

Ask Holy Spirit to assist you and provide the words and emotion. Make sure you are having the conversations that you need to have. Communicate, even when it's difficult. Create an expectation of when you will be ready to discuss the issue with your spouse. Don't drag things out to a point of creating even more frustration.

Stay in the conversation and address the issues that you've been avoiding. As difficult as this sounds for you as an avoider, it is the next step to take for your own growth and breakthrough.

Recognize that the health of your marriage is worth the discomfort of working through your issues together. Use phrases like, "Let's talk about this" or "our relationship and our marriage are important to me and we can work this out".

Solution/Suggested resources:

Determine who you are by recognizing your own communication "love style". We have experienced great success in sharing the "How we love" material, written by Milan and Kay Yerkovich. By taking the How We Love quiz, you will quickly determine which of the 6 styles you are. (Avoider, Pleaser, Vacillator, Controller, Victim, Connector). Once you determine your love style, you will be able to recognize how you respond and react during different situations and circumstances. The HWL material is a complete study in itself, so please make use of the quiz and utilize their material as you choose. www.Howwelove.com

Ephesians 4:15 *"But instead we will remain strong and always sincere in our love as we express the truth. All our direction and ministries will flow from Christ and lead us deeper into him, the anointed Head of his body, the church."*

1 Corinthians 3:16 *"Don't you realize that together you have become God's inner sanctuary and that the Spirit of God makes his permanent home in you?*

Escalation

How do I recognize it in myself?

You react negatively toward your spouse in a number of ways including sarcasm, name calling, threats and other forms of attack.

You respond to your spouse by arguing and increasing your level of intensity, so that the conversation gets more heated and more hosile.

What it looks like:

People who escalate get angrier as the discussion goes on, sometimes to the point of yelling or becoming violent.

Escalators have to get in the last word. You might try to make yourself feel better by making the other person feel worse, such as by bringing up other complaints.

Escalation takes higher steps in intensity. You may experience a sense of competition and a feeling that one of you has to win at the escalation!

What to do:

Step back and take a "time out". Recognize where you are in the conflict. Agree upon a time to discuss the issue when the emotion of the moment is gone and you're in a more peaceful state of mind. Don't go to bed angry or with the issue unresolved.

Be aware of the heightened emotion that is taking place and count to 10 if you need to. Do something to stop the flow of emotion so that you don't damage your relationship.

Solution/Suggested resources:

Ask Holy Spirit for guidance. Use phrases like: "Can we stop just a minute? This conversation is really important to me, so can we take some time to think and pray about it? How about setting aside some time after dinner so we can discuss it more together?" (The main idea is to decide upon some pre-determined time before the end of the day)

Proverbs 29:11 *"You can recognize fools by the way they give full vent to their rage and let their words fly! But the wise bite their tongues and hold back all they could say."*

Proverbs 18:6 *"A senseless man jumps headfirst into an argument; he's just asking for a beating for his reckless words."*

<u>Negative Interpretation</u>

How do I recognize it in myself?

You automatically believe or assign a specific motive to your spouse that is more negative than it really is. This is self-created because of your own emotion and experiences. This has little to do with your spouse's words or tone.

What it looks like:

When something your spouse says or does could be interpreted as either positive or negative. More often than not, you might get defensive at seemingly innocent questions, like "What did you do today?" A seemingly positive comment, like "You look nice tonight," may be taken negatively, to mean the person thinks you normally look terrible.

You spend a lot of time wondering whether there is a hidden (negative) message behind the things your spouse says or does.

What to do:

Ask Holy Spirit to guide you and assist in this process. Believe the best of your spouse. Many times our emotions and our "interpretation" of things are totally off because of our current situation, challenges or thoughts of the day. You become very selfish and disconnected from the reality of the actual communicated message.

Whenever your spouse says something that could be taken either way, positive or negative, assume the positive. Expect the best and ask questions for clarity if need be.

Solution/Suggested resources:

Phrases to use: "When you say/do (the thing that could be negatively interpreted), what do you mean by that?" or "Help me understand what you mean."

1 Corinthians 13:7 *"Love is a safe place of shelter, for it never stops believing the best for others. Love never takes failure as defeat, for it never gives up."*

Invalidate

How do I recognize it in myself?

It begins with a lack of awareness or sensitivity toward your spouse.

You process what you think you heard, versus what was actually said.

You may use subtle or direct insults of the thoughts, feelings, or character of your spouse.

You either directly or indirectly dismiss or minimize their comments or contributions to a conversation.

It may even include picking apart your spouse's feelings or point of view.

What it looks like:

You tell your spouse what they think or how they feel, instead of engaging or empathizing with them. You tell them that they shouldn't think or feel that way.

Instead of addressing your spouse's concerns, you declare that their concerns are not valid and therefore don't have to be dealt with.

Your first response is to try to "win" the argument, even when the facts are insignificant. You might change the meaning of what they said in an attempt to manipulate them.

Invalidation often happens because you assume that there's no way you could be wrong; therefore, when someone else disagrees with you, they must be wrong.

If your spouse introduces something to discuss with you and then ends up apologizing for bringing it up, you know that you're an invalidator.

What to do:

Recall our goal for mutual understanding. Instead of trying to win the argument, try to understand your spouse's point of view.

If the argument involves insignificant details, step back and recognize the value of letting go of minor details.

Empathize and consider things from your spouse's perspective. Try to feel what they are feeling and talk it through in a caring and understanding way.

Be humble enough to realize that they might be right, you might be wrong. God is using His gift of your spouse to help you see things from a different perspective.

Solutions/Suggested resources:

Phrases to use: "Help me understand why you feel that way." "What I hear you saying is… (In your own words, restate what you understand them to mean)."

Romans 12:16 *"Live happily together in a spirit of harmony, and be as mindful of another's worth as you are your own. Don't live with a lofty mind-set, thinking you are too important to serve others, but be willing to do menial tasks and identify with those who are humble minded. Don't be smug or even think for a moment that you know it all."*

James 4:6 *"But he continues to pour out more and more grace upon us. For it says, God resists you when you are proud but continually pours out grace when you are humble."*

1 Peter 5:5 *"In the same way, the younger ones should willingly support the leadership of the elders. In every relationship, each of you must wrap around yourself the apron of a humble servant, because God resists you when you are proud but multiplies grace and favor when you are humble."*

Positive steps forward

The first step in making any change in your life is to have some level of personal awareness. Your awareness and recognition of your own individual communication style will lead you to a better understanding of how you interact with others, including your spouse. The "negative" styles will turn into positives, as you work together to better understand how you communicate. Your ability to recognize how and why you communicate the way you do will allow for many more successes.

Questions/Activities/Activations/

You have just read through a number of significant ideas and possible confirmations about WHO you are in your communication style. It could be humbling and possibly challenging, as you work through some of your own emotions and validations. Ask Holy Spirit for clarification on any or all of these, as He continues to draw you closer to Him in the process.

Question One: Ask Holy Spirit if you are exhibiting any of these patterns.

Withdrawal or Avoid:

Escalate:

Negatively Interpret:

Invalidate:

Step Two: Now ask your spouse and have a conversation. Share how you are displaying any of these. Be caring and graceful as you discuss.

Question Two: What do these bible verses teach us about negative communication patterns?

1 Corinthians 13:7 *"Love is a safe place of shelter, for it never stops believing the best for others. Love never takes failure as defeat, for it never gives up."*

Matthew 5:22 *"But I'm telling you, if you hold anger in your heart toward a fellow believer, you are subject to judgment. And whoever demeans and insults a fellow believer is answerable to the congregation. And whoever calls down curses upon a fellow believer is in danger of being sent to a fiery hell."*

Proverbs 29:11 *"You can recognize fools by the way they give full vent to their rage and let their words fly. But the wise bite their tongues and hold back all they could say."*

Ephesians 4:15 *"But instead we will remain strong and always sincere in our love as we express the truth. All our direction and ministries will flow from Christ and lead us deeper into him, the anointed Head of his body, the church."*

Activities: Invest some time to learn more about your own strengths and identity. In learning about who we are and how God created us, we become aware of how we complement others. One meaningful assessment for determining your own personal strengths is by taking the Strengthsfinder test through Gallup and Tom Rath. You'll determine your top 5 strengths from a list of 34, uncovering things you may already know. This will provide an opportunity for affirmation of those strengths as you share with your spouse. Recognizing the strengths in each other can be a wonderful experience. It can be one that will open new doors of conversation as well as understanding how God uniquely brought you together! The free test can be found at this web address https://high5test.com/strengthsfinder-free/

There are amazing tools available to help us understand our personalities, behavior styles, love languages, strengths, and more.

One of our favorite tools is DISC, which helps us understand that there are four basic behavior styles.

D-Dominance. **D's** are the get-er-done achievers.

I-Influence. **I's** love to inspire and entertain people.

S-Steadiness. **S's** are loyal connectors.

C-Conscientious. **C's** love information, details, and getting things right.

D's and C's are more task-oriented, while I's and S's are people oriented. Each style has different needs, goals, and concerns. For more information please visit https://www.truity.com/test/disc-personality-test This is one of a number of free tests to get you started.

Activation: As you share time with your spouse this week, be intentional about recognizing these negative patterns and communicate what you're feeling and sensing. Ask Holy Spirit to assist you and provide you the discernment you need to be effective in your own communication!

Notes and ideas:

Chapter 6: Communication in Action
"Working through conflict"

Clear communication will create productive patterns for mutual understanding, but what about the times when things don't go according to plan? No matter where you are in your marriage, you will have conflict. The idea of conflict isn't something we mention in our wedding vows, but conflict can prove to be a meaningful catalyst for a healthy marriage. Conflict typically comes when there is a misunderstanding, unmet expectations or a lack of clear communication. Think about your own examples of conflict. How did it make you feel, how did you deal with it? We shared some familiar verses back in Chapter 2 on conflict, but James 4:1-3 offers another great reference to how we struggle in our relationships…*"What is the cause of your conflicts and quarrels with each other? Doesn't the battle begin inside of you as you fight to have your own way and fulfill your own desires? You jealously want what others have so you begin to see yourself as better than others. You scheme with envy and harm others to selfishly obtain what you crave—that's why you quarrel and fight. And all the time you don't obtain what you want because you won't ask God for it! If you ask, you won't receive it for you're asking with corrupt motives, seeking only to fulfill your own selfish desires."* Allow those words to soak in a bit and ask Holy Spirit for His guidance. Much of our struggle is from within. Most of the issues around conflict begin with our own selfishness. How do these words from James speak to you, as you remember those times of conflict? Let's work through some of the basics on conflict and respond diligently, addressing it early and often.

Biblical Truth: James 4:1-3, Matthew 7:4-5, 12, Proverbs 15:1, 19: 11, Ephesians 4:2-3, 4:26-27, Matthew 18:15-17, Romans 12:17-19, Matthew 19:26.

SUCCESSFUL steps forward

We know that conflict will come into your marriage, it's normal. How you respond to conflict will either produce success or frustrations along the way. There is some remarkable information that has been gathered by Drs. John and Julie Gottman of the Gottman institute. They have decades of experience and numerous studies conducted on all facets of relationships, including marriages. Their research results can identify which couples will succeed and those that will deteriorate with an astounding accuracy rate of 95%, just by how they handle conflict. They have identified 4 relational habits, or as they refer to them as "the Four Horsemen". Being able to identify them in your conflict discussions is a necessary first step to eliminating them and replacing them with healthy, productive communication patterns.

"THE FOUR HORSEMEN"

Criticism, Contempt, Defensiveness and Stonewalling

CRITICISM: Verbally attacking personality or character - Criticizing your partner is different than offering a critique or voicing a complaint. We can all think of times when we have offered our own suggestions or opinions to our spouse. This is deeper. Criticism, knowingly or not, is an attack on your partner's character. The problem with criticism is that when it becomes consistent or regular, it paves the way for the other relational habits. This may escalate into a pattern of criticism with greater frequency and intensity, which eventually leads to contempt.

Antidote: Talk about how you're feeling using "I" statements and express a positive response or need from your spouse. (Matthew 7:12) Empathy is a great equalizer if you recognize the need to "treat others as you'd like to be treated". Share YOUR feelings and express your own emotions. Avoid defining motives or your spouse's intention and feelings.

CONTEMPT: Attacking sense of self with intent to insult or abuse. When you communicate contempt, you treat others with disrespect. It may look like mocking them with sarcasm, ridicule, name calling or using body language such as eye-rolling or scoffing. Your intent is to make your spouse feel despised and worthless. Contempt goes far beyond criticism. Criticism attacks character, contempt assumes a position of moral superiority. Gottman studies have shown that contempt is the single greatest predictor of divorce.

Antidote: Build a culture of appreciation. Remind yourself of your partner's positive qualities and find gratitude for positive actions. (Proverbs 19:11) There may be a level of understanding to offer grace to your spouse in the situation. Begin with clear communication by asking some good thoughtful questions. Those questions should lead both of you into a more productive conversation for mutual understanding.

DEFENSIVENESS: We've all been defensive, but this habit seems to be upfront and always present when relationships are struggling. Being defensive is about victimizing yourself to ward off a perceived attack. When you feel unjustly accused, you look for excuses and assume the victim role so that your spouse will back off. This strategy is rarely successful. Excuses let your spouse know that you don't take their accusations seriously and that there is no way you're taking responsibility for your role in the matter.

Antidote: Take responsibility. Accept your partner's perspective and offer an apology for any wrongdoing. (Matthew 7:4-5) One of the biggest challenges we face during a conflict, disagreement or misunderstanding is the recognition of our own contribution to the conflict. Accountability and recognition of your own involvement may be the biggest step you can take for a successful outcome.

STONEWALLING: It is the opposite of connecting. It is the act of withdrawing to avoid conflict and convey emotion. They shut down, and simply stop responding to you. Rather than confronting, your spouse will tune out, turn away, act busy in some other activity, or engage in an obsessive or distracting behavior. Over time, this behavior may create a level of acceptance and normalcy. Stonewalling isn't easy to stop; it can easily become a habit. Remember, this is a result of feeling physiologically flooded or being triggered by some traumatic event or emotion from their past. If your spouse is in a state of stonewalling, they may not even be in a state where they can discuss things rationally. Recognizing their place of being overwhelmed may allow you to step away, take a break and come back to discuss the issue later. Ephesians 4:26-27, *"But don't let the passion of your emotions lead you to sin! Don't let anger control you or be fuel for revenge, not for even a day. Don't give the slanderous accuser, the devil, an opportunity to manipulate you!"*

Antidote: Allow for some self-soothing, take a break and spend that time doing something distracting. Be sure to share that you are willing and interested in discussing the issues, but that you would ask for their understanding and for a plan to discuss later. (Proverbs 3:5-6) May offer some comfort, as well as (Matthew 19:26). We have an advocate, our High Priest that intercedes for us. Be confident in the presence of Holy Spirit and lean on Him.

Don't take the bait

One of the most effective ways the enemy takes advantage of us is by tempting us with offense. When you feel the need to lash out, react or just take offense to something, DON'T take the bait. The enemy wants to stir you up in your flesh and tempt you *to bite on the need for justice*. Romans 12:17-19 provides a strong antidote for offense. *"Never hold a grudge or try to get even, but plan your life around the noblest way to benefit others. Do your best to live as everybody's friend. Beloved, don't be obsessed with taking revenge, but leave that to God's righteous justice. For the Scriptures say: "Vengeance is mine, and I will repay," says the Lord."* If we could only remember these words during those times of frustration and our temptation to selfishly lash out. God wants to take care of us and protect us, especially in our time of need.

Proverbs 15:1 suggests that we *"Respond gently when you are confronted and you'll defuse the rage of another. Responding with sharp, cutting words will only make it worse. Don't you know that being angry can ruin the testimony of even the wisest of men?"*

Ask for additional help

The goal for effective communication is mutual understanding, not just to bring others into the conversation to help you present your side of the story. You may find a need during challenging times in your marriage for additional help or assistance. Recognize that there is biblical guidance for dealing with sin and conflict. Matthew 18:15-17 says, *"If your fellow believer sins against you, you must go to that one privately and attempt to resolve the matter. If he responds, your relationship is restored. But if his heart is closed to you, then go to him again, taking one or two others with you. You'll be fulfilling what the Scripture teaches when it says, 'Every word may be verified by the testimony of two or three witnesses.' And if he refuses to listen, then share the issue with the congregation in hopes of restoration. If he still refuses to respond, even to the church, then you must disregard him as though he were an outsider, on the same level as an unrepentant sinner."* These verses reference two people dealing with an issue, so it may include the assistance of friends or your small group. Whatever assistance you seek, God wants the best for you and will provide guidance of Holy Spirit, as you seek Him first.

Conflict will come

There is no question as to whether or not we will face conflict; it comes down to how we respond to the conflict. A powerful healthy couple will see conflict as an opportunity to deal with the issues that are trying to tear them apart. Satan has a focus on creating havoc in our marriages; don't let it happen to you. When you sense the conflict, take aim and take action.

Take a moment and receive comfort in these strong words from Paul to the church at Ephesus. Ephesians 4:2-3 says, *"With tender humility and quiet patience, always demonstrate gentleness and generous love toward one another, especially toward those who may try your patience. Be faithful to guard the sweet harmony of the Holy Spirit among you in the bonds of peace."* We are blessed to have these words to encourage us, directing us in the way we should go. Pray and ask for Holy Spirit's presence and His guidance throughout any conflict. Your marriage will grow towards oneness and others will see Christ in both of you!

Questions/Activities/Activations/

Question 1: Think about conflict in your own family of origin and describe how it was handled. Ask Holy Spirit how to deal with conflict in your marriage today?

Question 2: What is your view of conflict, something to avoid OR something to deal with and recognize as an opportunity to build connection with your spouse?

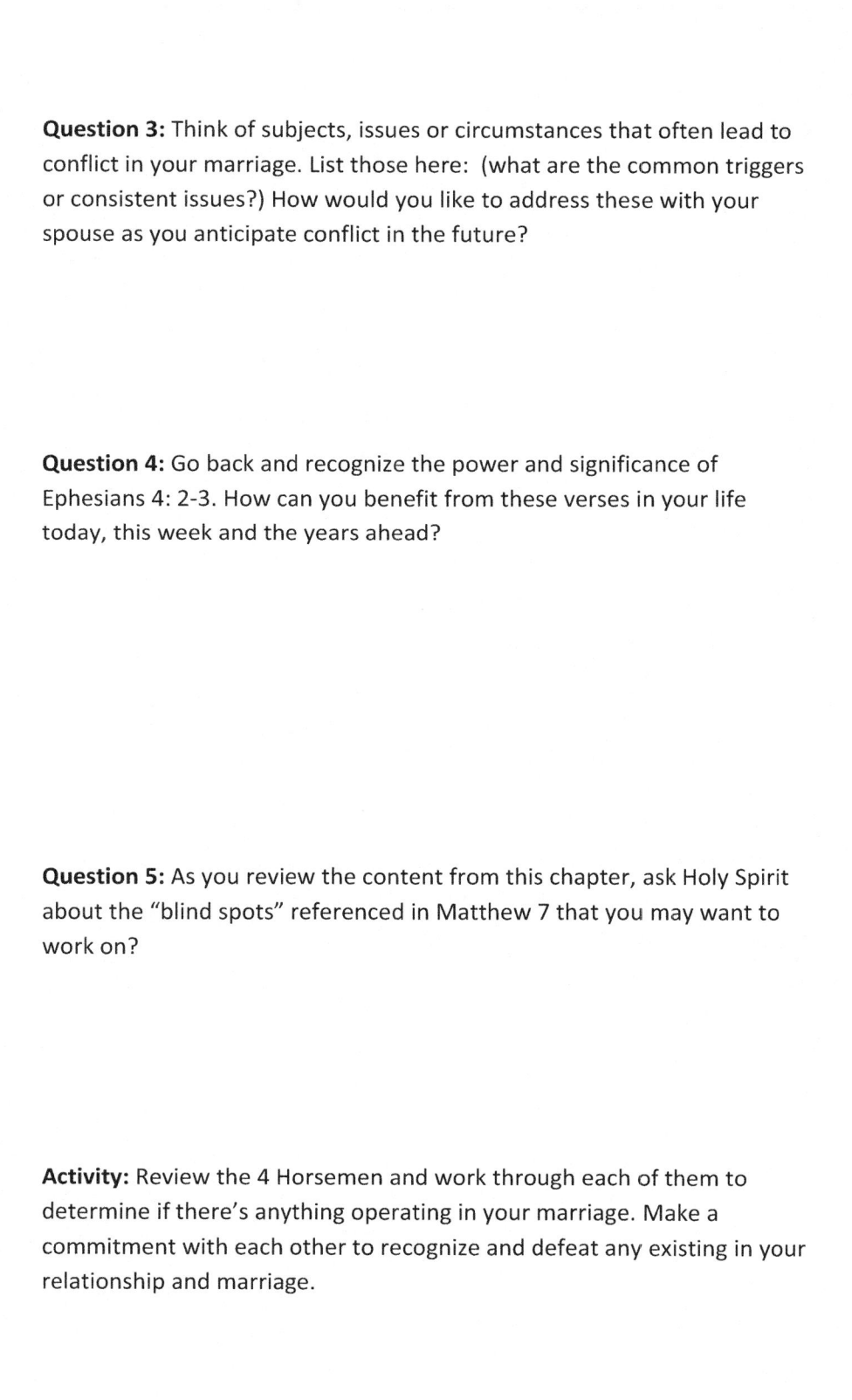

Question 3: Think of subjects, issues or circumstances that often lead to conflict in your marriage. List those here: (what are the common triggers or consistent issues?) How would you like to address these with your spouse as you anticipate conflict in the future?

Question 4: Go back and recognize the power and significance of Ephesians 4: 2-3. How can you benefit from these verses in your life today, this week and the years ahead?

Question 5: As you review the content from this chapter, ask Holy Spirit about the "blind spots" referenced in Matthew 7 that you may want to work on?

Activity: Review the 4 Horsemen and work through each of them to determine if there's anything operating in your marriage. Make a commitment with each other to recognize and defeat any existing in your relationship and marriage.

Solutions/Activities/ Suggested resources:

*Take time to research the topic of conflict. You will find many references, resources and content pertaining to conflict. Recognize and embrace your differences. Read books, take additional classes and appreciate those things that brought you together. Go back to those differences and embrace your complements for future personal growth and love in your relationship.

*Establish your own "rules of engagement" when it comes to conflict. We've discussed it earlier, but recognize the time when you need to pause, collect yourselves and plan for meaningful conversation later in the day. Taking a "time out" will allow for your emotions to level out. This will give you awareness to slow down and process the details in your own time, before rejoining the conversation.

*Recognize that communication is 55% non-verbal. There are as many as 9 non-verbal communication types that all play into our ability to effectively communicate. 38% of communication is vocal or tonal and 7% are your actual words. Understand that much of what you communicate is through your tone and non-verbal body language. It's an amazing statistic we all need to be more aware of. Be sensitive and tune into the significance of every method we express, OR don't express.

*Inclusion of Four Horsemen has been approved, with attribution to Drs John and Julie Gottman and the Gottman Institute. Thank you Gottman Institute for all that you've done for relationships and marriages.

Chapter 7: Forgiveness

One of the most powerful examples of love, care and understanding in a relationship can be expressed through the gift of forgiveness. If you've been in any kind of relationship, you know the pain that can come from being hurt or misunderstood. You may also know the **life giving power** of forgiveness, as you have forgiven others and others have forgiven you along the way. We have found this topic to be one of the most influential, in course corrections within a marriage. Offering forgiveness can be the most powerful and meaningful step you can take for moving forward in a healthy relationship. It lets the other person off the hook and puts a stop to you keeping score, or tracking other minor items within the relationship. Forgiveness is for the forgiver, it is for YOU. Jesus is our perfect example of forgiveness, as God offered His plan of salvation through His one and only Son. The entire Bible is the story of God's plan of redemption for us, as we read the prophetic messages in the Old Testament. The example of God's love for us is shared multiple times throughout the Bible, as He forgives His people over and over again. In the New Testament as Jesus' ministry begins, He again shares story after story of forgiveness. One of the most powerful depictions comes in the form of the story of the rich ruler in Matthew 18:21-35, as Peter is asking "how many times must I forgive my fellow believer?" It is a great reminder for all of us, the significance of forgiveness and the example we are to follow.

Jesus answered, "Not seven times, Peter, but seventy times seven times! The lessons of forgiveness in heaven's kingdom realm can be illustrated like this: *"There once was a king who had servants who had borrowed money from the royal treasury. He decided to settle accounts with each of them. As he began the process, it came to his attention that one of his servants owed him one billion dollars. So he summoned the servant before him and said to him, Pay me what you owe me. When his servant was unable to repay his debt, the king ordered that he be sold as a slave along with his wife and children and every possession they owned as payment toward his debt. The servant threw himself facedown at his master's feet and begged for mercy. Please be patient with me. Just give me more time and I will repay you all that I owe. Upon hearing his pleas, the king had compassion on his servant, and released him, and forgave his entire debt. No sooner had the servant left when he met one of his fellow servants, who owed him twenty thousand dollars. He seized him by the throat and began to choke him, saying, you'd better pay me right now everything you owe me! His fellow servant threw himself facedown at his feet and begged, please be patient with me. If you'll just give me time, I will repay you all that is owed. But the one who had his debt forgiven stubbornly refused to forgive what was owed him. He had his fellow servant thrown into prison and demanded he remain there until he repaid the debt in full. When his associates saw what was going on, they were outraged and went to the king and told him the whole story. The king said to him, you scoundrel! Is this the way you respond to my mercy? Because you begged me, I forgave you the massive debt that you owed me. Why didn't you show the same mercy to your fellow servant that I showed to you? In a fury of anger, the king turned him over to the prison guards to be tortured until all his debt was repaid. In this same way, my heavenly Father will deal with any of you if you do not release forgiveness from your heart toward your fellow believer."* The story shared here is one that needs to be read in its entirety as a reminder for all of us. The idea is to understand the hypocrisy of this story. We have all received forgiveness of our sin from Father God, but fail to forgive others?

Biblical Truth: Matthew 18:15, 21-35, Proverbs 19:11, Ephesians 4:31-32, Romans 12:19, Acts 3:19

WHY FORGIVE?

Aside from the obvious story above, we are to forgive because He first forgave us! God's example of forgiveness is the benchmark set for all of mankind. Ephesians 4:31-32 provides additional encouragement and direction for why we are to forgive. *"Lay aside bitter words, temper tantrums, revenge, profanity, and insults. But instead be kind and affectionate toward one another. Has God graciously forgiven you? Then graciously forgive one another in the depths of Christ's love."*

MORE BIBLICAL TRUTH ON FORGIVENESS

In addition to the reference in Ephesians above, the bible provides a number of great references to forgiveness.

Proverbs 19:11 shares... *"An understanding person demonstrates patience, for mercy means holding your tongue. When you are insulted, be quick to forgive and forget it, for you are virtuous when you overlook an offense."*

Matthew 18:15 describes the ease of offering forgiveness with other believers, including your spouse. *"If your fellow believer sins against you, you must go to that one privately and attempt to resolve the matter. If he responds, your relationship is restored."*

Matthew 5:23-24 *"If you are presenting a gift before the altar and suddenly you remember a quarrel you have with a fellow believer, leave your gift there in front of the altar and go at once to apologize to the one who is offended. Then, after you have reconciled, come to the altar and present your gift."*

When you recognize that you have said something wrong or you have hurt your spouse with your words or action, taking the initiative and asking for forgiveness before something has time to fester can really deepen your relationship, trust and mutual respect. Breakthrough often comes after forgiveness, as we've experienced many times. Experiences develop into statements like, "I want to forgive new things". I want to forgive things that are happening now, not from the past. "Forgiving things from the past are those things that I obviously haven't completely forgiven."

Recognizing where you are in the process of forgiveness is a great starting point. Read through some definitions of what forgiveness is and what it isn't.

Defining Forgiveness:

1. **Forgiveness is** an intentional, thoughtful and deliberate decision to release feelings of vengeance and resentment. Forgiveness is all about the forgiver. The person being forgiven may not even know of the issue. It is about you getting rid of negative feelings. Through the guidance of Holy Spirit, forgiveness is a conscious choice for all of us.

2. **Forgiveness** involves asking Holy Spirit for His peace, not justice. Forgiveness is irrespective of whether or not the person is deserving of your forgiveness. Forgiveness is separate and distinct from justice. The person who hurt you may never receive punishment or incur any consequences for their action. This fact should not prevent you from living in the freedom God has for you.

3. **Forgiveness** is a process that takes time, prayer, and effort to achieve. It CAN be something that happens "right now", as you release those emotions to Jesus. Forgiveness is for you, a decision you make for your own needs and experience. Read Ephesians 4:32

4. **Forgiveness is** an empowering action for you to identify your pain and begin the healing process. Forgiveness involves acknowledging that you have incurred the pain, but move intentionally beyond the pain to eliminate your suffering. Ask Holy Spirit to provide the steps necessary along the path toward pain relief and healing.

5. **Forgiveness is** a significant process for achieving peace of mind and happiness. It means letting go of things for Jesus to care for, which leads to freedom and a peace of mind for you. The act of forgiveness increases happiness and happy people are more likely to forgive.

6. **Forgiveness is** a way to cultivate empathy. Place yourself in the person's shoes that hurt you. Pray and ask The Lord to help you feel or imagine the remorse and distress felt by the other person. Once you are empathetic, forgiveness is a much easier and meaningful process.

7. **Forgiveness is** stress reducing. Forgiveness improves health. It can decrease blood pressure, heart rate, and stress. Reducing stress can help you physically, mentally, emotionally and spiritually.

8. **Forgiveness is** a way to connect with others. It is a command from Father God. When you forgive, you feel more positive toward others. Jesus will be seen in your forgiveness. It can help repair relationships, resolve conflicts and maintain stronger, more satisfying relationships, including marriage. Read Acts 3:19

AND what it's not:

1. **Forgiveness is not** forgetting. Make use of the memory as a benefit, to remind you of the commitment you've made to continue to forgive. Ask Jesus for His continued support.

2. **Forgiveness is not** condoning, accepting, excusing, enabling, enforcing, or encouraging bad behavior. As we forgive through His power, we are saying the offender is wrong. We do not condone or approve of their action. Forgiveness does not imply that what they did to us was alright. Your forgiveness does not erase the harm caused or encourage it to happen again.

3. **Forgiveness is not** ignoring. When someone's actions have been detrimental to you, it is not healthy to ignore what happened. Negative emotions will slowly take their toll on you and require you to deal with the wrong that has been done to you. Ask Jesus for His help.

4. **Forgiveness is not** being naïve or denying the action. Denying the past is difficult, dishonest, and unhealthy for any of us. To forgive, we need acknowledge the occurrence and the pain and leave it at the feet of Jesus.

Forgiveness is a great step along the path to healing. Ask Holy Spirit to protect you and guide you through this healing process.

5. **Forgiveness is not** waiting for someone to acknowledge their wrongdoing, repent or apologize. The person who caused you pain doesn't even have to feel badly about doing it. Forgiveness is irrespective of the person that harmed you or their state of mind. The act of forgiving is a blessing to you, as you release them to Jesus, creating a more harmonious and peaceful atmosphere for you and your surroundings.

6. **Forgiveness is not neglecting justice.** Forgiveness and justice may not occur simultaneously. Forgiveness does not remove the offender from legal accountability. Remember what it says in Romans 12: 19 *"Vengeance is mine and I will repay."*

7. **Forgiveness is not reconciliation**. You are forgiving someone who did you wrong, forgiving them. Reconciling takes two people and the guidance of Holy Spirit with two different processes. Reconciling cannot be achieved unless the victim forgives and the offender repents. Forgiveness is a necessary step on the road to reconciliation, but forgiving someone does not mean that you have an interest or are willing to reconcile.

8. **Forgiveness is not a two-way conversation**. Forgiveness is one-sided. It is all about you, the forgiver. Even if the offender never knows anything about your act of forgiving them, you will still reap the rewards of improving your mental, emotional, and spiritual health. God's desire is for you to live in the freedom that Christ died for. Ask Holy Spirit who you are to forgive and begin to celebrate the power of forgiveness in your life today!

Statements on forgiveness have been adapted and modified from Psychology today.

Questions/Activities/Activations:

Answer questions 1-4 on your own, then with your spouse, as you prepare and anticipate time with your small group. Remember to be still and know that He has a great plan for you during this study. What is Holy Spirit saying to you? What are you seeing, hearing or sensing? Allow Him to guide you in the process.

Question One: Review the list of "what forgiveness is not". Which of those do you have trouble applying to your own life, as well as in your marriage? Talk about them with your spouse.

Question Two: Those that you struggle with, take time to recognize why. Discuss with your spouse and ask for guidance from Holy Spirit. Why do I struggle with____? What makes____so difficult for me to deal with?

Question Three: List a few things that you think make it difficult for you to forgive others, your spouse?

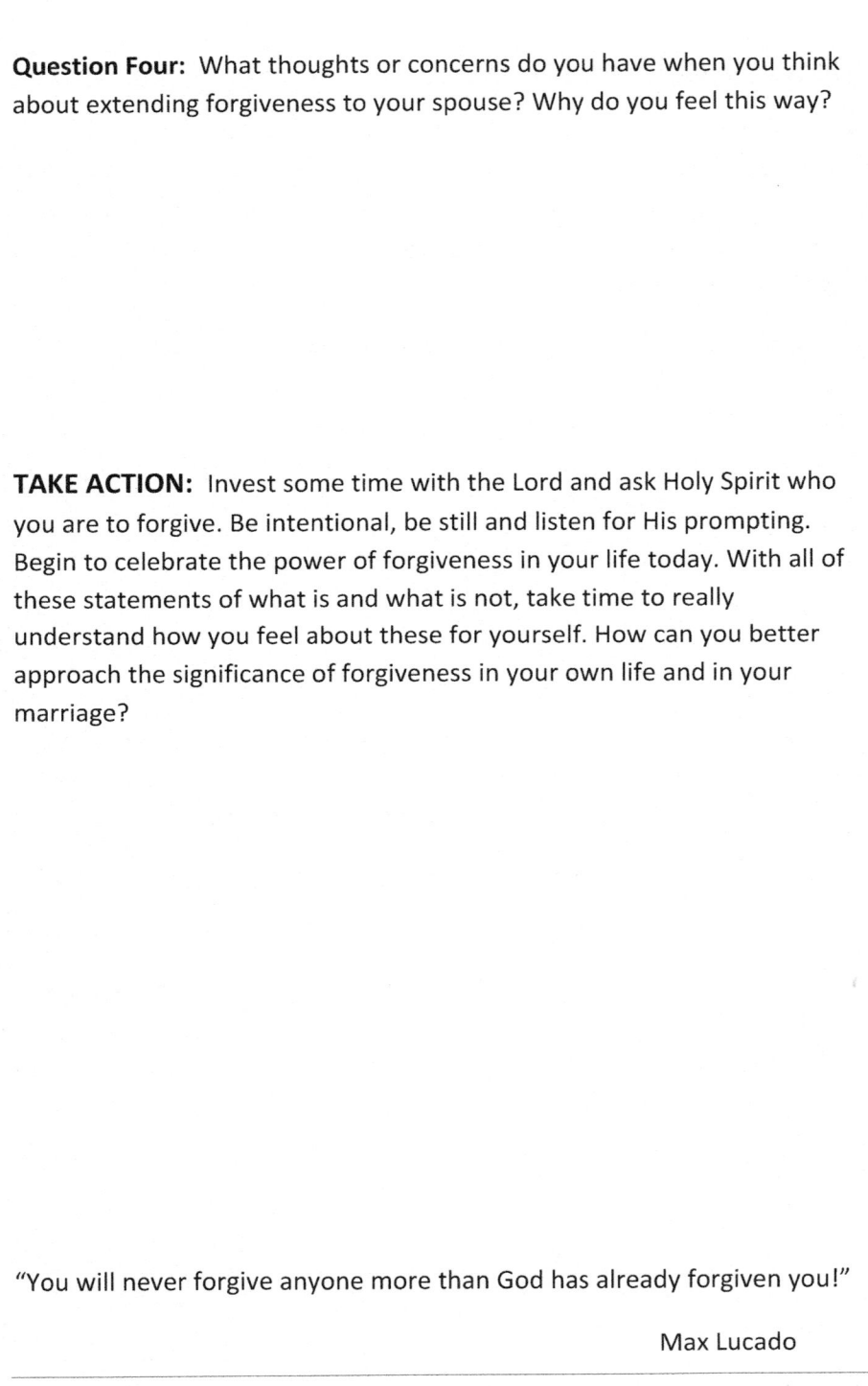

Question Four: What thoughts or concerns do you have when you think about extending forgiveness to your spouse? Why do you feel this way?

TAKE ACTION: Invest some time with the Lord and ask Holy Spirit who you are to forgive. Be intentional, be still and listen for His prompting. Begin to celebrate the power of forgiveness in your life today. With all of these statements of what is and what is not, take time to really understand how you feel about these for yourself. How can you better approach the significance of forgiveness in your own life and in your marriage?

"You will never forgive anyone more than God has already forgiven you!"

Max Lucado

Chapter 8: Activating Forgiveness

As we experience a life of offering forgiveness, there is a great sense of responsibility to share in the steps for success. Please read in Colossians chapter 3:13 about the significance of forgiveness. *"Tolerate the weaknesses of those in the family of faith, forgiving one another in the same way you have been graciously forgiven by Jesus Christ. If you find fault with someone, release this same gift of forgiveness to them."* We have so many wonderful examples, life stories and instructions from the Bible. Take confidence in the instruction that they all provide and be encouraged. In our weakness He can be strong, in and through each one of us. Ask Jesus for His strength to move you forward from your pain, toward the glorious gift of forgiveness.

Your decision to forgive and the process of forgiveness begin with a soft heart and a place of humility, guided by Holy Spirit. Taking action with your spouse looks like scheduling time with each other, as you work through issues of forgiveness. You may experience some real heartfelt emotion as you step through this together, so don't be surprised that this exercise takes a little longer than just reading the content and discussing the questions together. These steps have proven to bring significant change and have produced real resurrection in many couple's lives. Your experience will be uniquely your own and will be dependent on your level of intimacy and transparency with each other.

KEY POINT: As you begin, please recognize that there is a very big difference between saying I'm sorry and asking for forgiveness. Asking for forgiveness involves the other person and elicits a response from them to offer it up. Just saying "I'm sorry" isn't enough. It certainly shares the emotion, but doesn't quite get to the point of mutual understanding and respect for the action that is about to take place.

ONE:

Prepare yourself and ask for help, as it does in Psalm 139:23-24. *"God, I invite your searching gaze into my heart. Examine me through and through and find out everything that may be hidden within me. Put me to the test and sift through all my anxious cares. See if there is any path of pain I'm walking in, and lead me back to your glorious, everlasting way— the path that brings me back to you."*

Asking Holy Spirit to search you will prompt your thinking and your response to Him, so be sure to write down as many things that come to mind that you want to confess to Him.

1.

2.

3.

4.

TWO:

In your own quiet time with The Lord, confess each of these to Him and ask for forgiveness. 1 John 1:9 provides great direction for us. *"But if we freely admit our sins when his light uncovers them, he will be faithful to forgive us every time. God is just to forgive us our sins because of Christ, and he will continue to cleanse us from all unrighteousness."* Confessing your own sins to God will provide openness for forgiving others, including your spouse.

*You might say…"Lord, please forgive me of my own selfishness. I have failed to recognize my need for you, the needs of my spouse and my family. I have been so focused on myself that I have failed to recognize and love others as I should. Thank you for your forgiveness."

THREE:

Invite your spouse to join you, without any distractions and confess each of these issues that you've listed, one at a time. The goal is to simply confess to each other what you have done. Give your spouse time to share each issue, expressing emotion, pain and any disappointment they feel. The listener is to listen humbly, create a safe environment and allow them to release all that they have to share without judgment.

***You might say**..."I need to confess to you that I have put much more time and effort into my work than I have into our relationship and I know this has hurt you. I ask you to forgive me for not being more attentive and understanding. I want to know more about how you're feeling and how I have hurt you and caused you pain in this. Please forgive me..."

FOUR:

Now is the time to ask for forgiveness for each item specifically. Be sure to avoid saying I'm sorry or I apologize, as they are in the form of a statement. Asking your spouse for forgiveness in a repentant and sincere way will bring both of you into the process and a place of vulnerability for you.

***You might say**... "Will you please forgive me for the way I treated you? I behaved in a way that I know was wrong and I realize I hurt you." Asking your spouse for forgiveness opens the door to a return response. You have now engaged yourself in the process, which offers an opportunity for clear understanding and awareness for both parties.

FIVE:

After your spouse has asked for forgiveness, return their request with grace and forgive them as they have requested. Remember the significance of forgiveness that we learned in chapter 7 and the power of forgiveness that Christ has offered all of us, freely.

***You might say**…"Yes I was hurt by the way you behaved and I can see that you recognize the hurt you caused me. I will forgive you."

This process can be a bit awkward and uncomfortable, but as you work your way through the steps and the items you've listed, your relationship will be enhanced and your level of intimacy and vulnerability will increase. Breakthrough can occur when you share honest and open communication with one another. Again, ask Holy Spirit for His guidance. Forgiveness is powerful and will have a dramatic effect on your marriage. This may be the first time you've experienced this level of openness and offering forgiveness, so it may be difficult and it does take practice. Having a healthy marriage takes work and having these types of conversations will provide opportunity for additional practice as you experience life together. Remember your own brokenness, the power of God's love and His forgiveness and grace on your life. This process will become easier over time and will be more spontaneous as you grow in your faith and in your relationship.

Biblical Truth: Colossians 3:13, Psalm 139:23-24, 1 John 1:9, Psalm 51:4

Questions/Activities/Activations

You have a very unique opportunity to share in these questions below. Ask Holy Spirit to guide you through each one, as you answer them on your own and then with each other. You may be surprised at the conversation and additional questions that come from your time together. Share some of those thoughts here.

Question One: Share how you felt as you experienced the process. What was the most difficult thing you experienced?

Question Two: Throughout the process, was it more difficult to offer forgiveness OR to ask for forgiveness? Why?

Question Three: As you asked and offered forgiveness with each other, was there anything that came to mind or made it difficult to proceed?

Question Four: What steps can you take to make this process easier and incorporate it as a practice throughout your marriage?

Chapter 9: Commitment

We have been taught throughout much of our lives that there is *a quid pro quo* to life, haven't we? "If I give you something of value, you will give me something in return". It is a model of give and take. We follow this understood practice from our life experience, which in turn sets an expectation of how we respond. The example of this in our daily lives is what we often experience in a contractual relationship. We have a contract and agree to work with our utilities, phone, and electricity providers in what they will provide us. I agree to pay you for the service you provide as long as the service is acceptable and meets my standards. When I'm dissatisfied or done with the service I break the contract and move on to another provider. Unfortunately this understanding and life example has crept its way into our marriages too. Society today has been trained and conditioned to accept this kind of contractual relationship. Marriages have become as easy to break as the agreements with our service providers. As Christians, we must be more aware of the significance of God's covenantal relationship that He modeled for us. We must be committed to that same covenant relationship with each other.

Biblical Truth: Romans 5:10, Malachi 2:14, Mark 10:1-12

Daily application:

God's Covenant relationship

The practical application of this information will take you to a deeper appreciation for Holy Spirit's leading and teaching. Please remember to invite Him into the process and be prepared for what He has to say. You will be impressed with the dialog that you have, as you ask and wait for His response. With that said, take a look at one of the significant verses on forgiveness and reconciliation.

Romans 5:10 opens the conversation with God as our reconciler. *"So if while we were still enemies, God fully reconciled us to himself through the death of his Son, then something greater than friendship is ours. Now that we are at peace with God, and because we share in his resurrection life, how much more we will be rescued from sin's dominion!"*

Reconciliation comes from His irrevocable **covenants** with His people, as seen throughout the Bible. Five of the most significant covenants are as follows: *The Noahic Covenant, the Abrahamic Covenant, The Mosaic Covenant, the Davidic Covenant and the New Covenant.* These five covenants are crucial for understanding the story of the Bible and God's redemptive plan for all of us. These are covenantal not contractual, where man had to do something to receive His favor. These covenants were offered in spite of what His people did. The blessings of these covenants were based on His love and commitment to His people and the redemptive plan that He had for all of us from the very beginning. As we experience His love, commitment and covenant with us, He expects us to have a covenant relationship with our spouse. He provided the model for each one of us. It has been expressed throughout the Bible as an example for how we are to commit to one another in our marriage. The covenant relationship in a marriage is a powerful expression of His love for the entire world to see. Unfortunately our culture has completely turned this upside down. The opportunity to share a biblically based, covenant relationship is another powerful testimony of your marriage.

During the time of the Mosaic covenant, God expressed His anger and shared these words in Malachi 2:14*"You cry out, "Why doesn't the Lord accept my worship?" I'll tell you why! Because the Lord witnessed the vows you and your wife made when you were young. But you have been unfaithful to her, though she remained your faithful partner, the wife of your marriage vows."* God kept His covenant relationship with the people of Israel but they had forgotten Him, they had "strayed" and didn't remember their commitment to the relationship. God is serious about covenants. When we keep our covenants with each other, we love like God loves.

ACTIVATE Covenant in your marriage

Take a minute or two to think about your own covenant with each other. What does that look like for the two of you? Your level of commitment with each other will be different from others because it is yours. Take some initial steps and be intentional about your commitment with one another. Go beyond the vows you took during your wedding and think about the commitment that you make today and for the days ahead. The process may be as easy as reminding yourself of your commitment to holding each other accountable when times get tough, especially if you're hearing the divisive lies of the enemy. Stand firm in your identity in Jesus and recognize where those lies are coming from. Don't take the bait. **Don't listen to the distractions of this world that say you should quit or move on to someone else.** Your own awareness and thoughtful self-reflection will prove to be a daily reminder of God's commitment and covenant with you. Your spouse is a gift from God. Give thanks and appreciate the significance of His gift.

ACTIVE steps of commitment:

*Never mention the word divorce. Remind each other of your covenant marriage, especially when it comes to difficult times. Commitment leads to healthy conversations and trust, with the understanding that we are in this together.

*Write down your goals and put together a mission statement for your life together. The two of you have been brought together for greater things, serving the Kingdom. Share and determine what God's plan is for your life together.

*Avoid uncomfortable situations with the opposite sex. Becoming close friends or holding on to past friendships with the opposite sex are in opposition to your oneness.

*Flirting or having inappropriate emotional relationships with others of the opposite sex will cause harm and need to be avoided.

*Have consistent conversation with each other, nurturing your relationship and reminding each other of your commitment to a life-long love for one another. (In the absence of fact we make stuff up!)

*Recognize how each of you receives love and activate your love languages regularly.

No way out

The commitment you make to each other in your covenant relationship will promote a process of eliminating distractions and possible ways out of your marriage. You want to identify them now, as those alternatives won't become options if things get tough. Closing doors to other options will promote a deeper level of trust and understanding between the two of you. You may want to openly discuss what options you have thought about in your own experiences. Doors of *escape* might look like staying busy, getting caught up in work, being out with friends, hobbies or other activities that could take you away from each other. None of these are bad, but if any of them are used to avoid the real issues and run away from having healthy conversations, they could be seen as an open door. Eliminating those potential options is your commitment to one another saying I won't leave or become preoccupied with other things or distractions. Any of these could be recognized as a door to "the enemy", so whatever door you've left open, be mindful of what you're enabling and seek healing for items that may have entered in the past. This is an exercise that expresses that you are committed to each other and that you're committed to working on the issues and not walk away.

Contract or Covenant?

Earlier in the chapter we shared a number of thoughts on this very meaningful comparison. Don't miss the significance and don't miss the opportunity to commit to the power of this concept. The world would like you to believe that you're in a contractual relationship with your spouse. It says that everything is good, as long as you keep up your end of the agreement. If you're in an abusive relationship you will want to seek additional help and care. The teachings of the bible speak against abusive relationships and adultery. These sensitive issues need to be dealt with individually and with professional assistance. Working through issues in a committed, covenantal relationship will lead you to new levels of intimacy. It will promote more respect in your relationship as you work through seasons of difficulty and the simple issues you deal with throughout your marriage.

Questions/Activities/Activations/

Remember to be intentional about going through the questions in each chapter. Ask Holy Spirit to guide you through each one of the questions, as you answer them on your own and then with each other. Fully appreciate the process and recognize what He wants to do in your life and in your marriage.

Question One: As you read through the differences between a contract and covenant relationship, how would you define YOUR marriage and why?

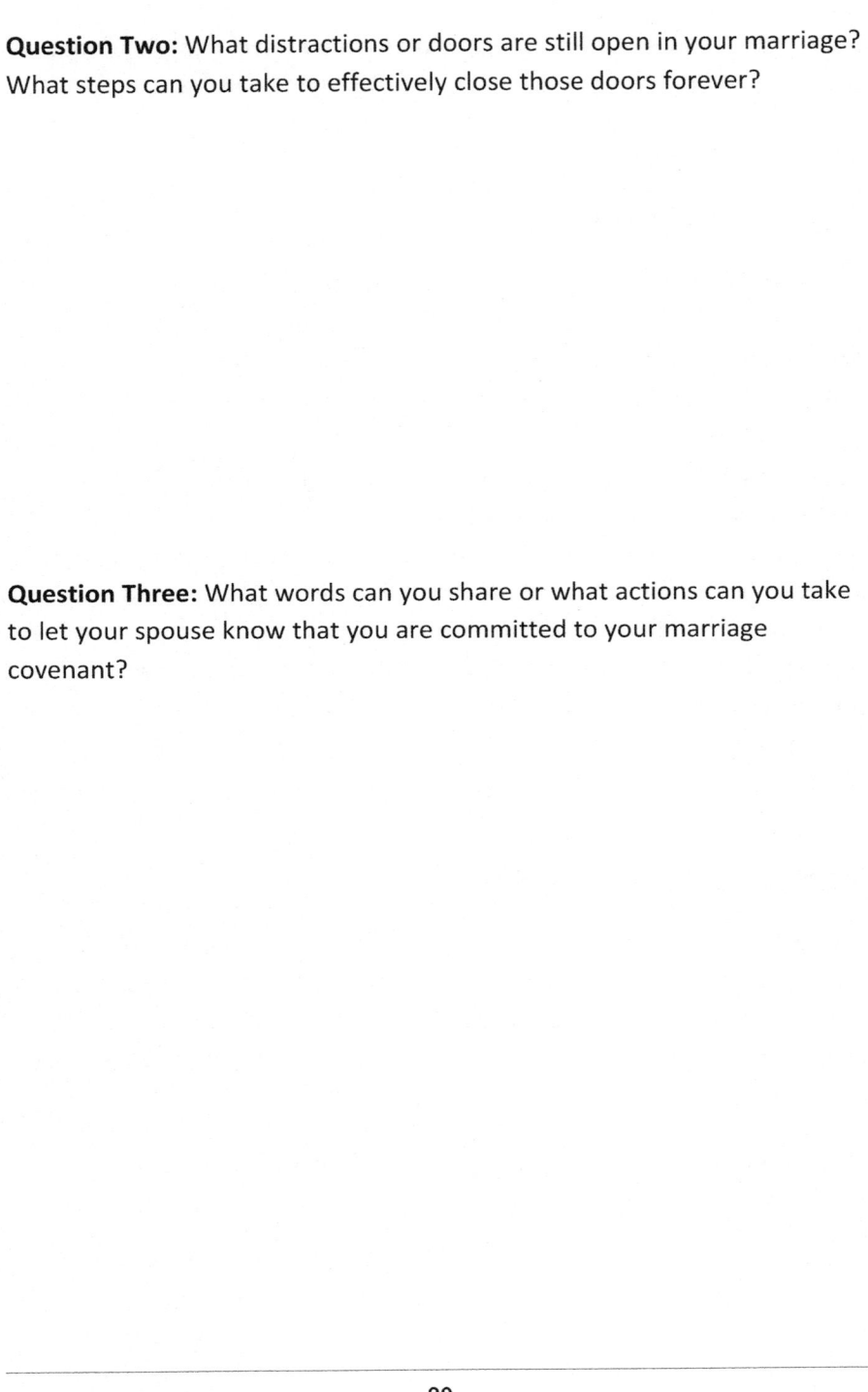

Question Two: What distractions or doors are still open in your marriage? What steps can you take to effectively close those doors forever?

Question Three: What words can you share or what actions can you take to let your spouse know that you are committed to your marriage covenant?

Question Four: Read Mark 10:6-9 and allow the words of Jesus to resonate, as he restates verses from Genesis. What is the significance and meaning of "joining together?"

Question Five: Describe your feelings and impressions of the relationship that God has with you? How is that example expressed in your marriage and with one another?

As we wrap up this chapter, we have found that the need to control and the FEAR that often comes from not being in control can be a big contributor to many of our relational issues. If that statement brings attention to an emotion in either one of you, this is a good time to discuss. "Do not be afraid" is written 365 times in the bible. There is a DAILY reminder from God to live every day without fear. When you release your fears to The Lord and let Him lead your marriage, you will find peace and the freedom that Jesus died for.

Notes and Ideas:

Chapter 10: Sharing Truth

There is so much power in the word of God as we read through the Bible. We are always impressed with how Holy Spirit guides us and speaks to each one of us in different ways. Sometimes the most powerful and yet simple ways He speaks TRUTH to us is through His word...

Proverbs 6:23 "For truth is a bright beam of light shining into every area of your life, instructing and correcting you to discover the ways to godly living."

Colossians 4:6 "Let every word you speak be drenched with grace and tempered with truth and clarity. For then you will be prepared to give a respectful answer to anyone who asks about your faith."

How can we make practical use of these biblical descriptions of truth? How can we relate and apply what we read in the Bible? The first step is to get into the word, read and recognize its relevance in our life today and every day.

We live in a very active and news-filled life. How do we recognize, believe in and share the truth with one another in our daily lives? Different forms of media, long trusted sources of news and information are in question and have seemed to push us to question just about everything. How do we nurture truth in our relationships and with our spouse? There are so many questions...The one thing that we CAN rely on is the love and TRUTH that comes from Father God, as we see below in Romans.

Romans 12:2 *"Stop imitating the ideals and opinions of the culture around you, but be inwardly transformed by the Holy Spirit through a total reformation of how you think. This will empower you to discern God's will as you live a beautiful life, satisfying and perfect in his eyes."*

These encouraging words are just as significant today as they were when Paul wrote them down for his audience in Rome. How will you incorporate them into your life? Ask Holy Spirit for His truth throughout your day and listen. He will provide clarity and meaningful guidance for truth, no matter where you are in a particular situation or circumstance.

Biblical Truth: Romans 12:2, 1 Corinthians 6:18, 7:27-29, 10:13, 13:4-7, Psalm 16:11, Psalm 103:10, Matthew 4:1-11, 19:5-6, Deuteronomy 14:2, Colossians 4:6, Proverbs 6:23

Daily application:

"UN Truth's" in marriage

What lies are you believing? What lies seem to be more evident in society today about marriage? How can we refute those lies and stand against them? Take time to read and discuss the list of lies you might be hearing and/or believing below.

   1. **"I married the wrong person"**

Just about everyone at some point in their marriage will have this thought. Once you believe this lie, the only things you notice about your spouse are the things you're not compatible with. It is God's will for you to stay married to your spouse. You made a commitment to them when God brought you together. Matthew 19:5-6 provides a great reminder. For this reason a man will leave his father and mother and live with his wife. *"And the two will become one flesh. From then on, they are no longer two, but united as one. So what God unites let no one divide!"* You didn't marry the wrong person; you married an imperfect person with a number of flaws, just like you. Make an intentional effort to invest in your marriage. The more active you are working on your marriage the less time you'll spend wondering about the "what if's". Learn to love your spouse well and do all you can to see them as God sees them.

2. "My marriage and our issues are different and unique"

Satan wants to isolate you and make you think that you're different and unique. He is the great deceiver and manipulator of truth. 1 Corinthians 10:13 says *"We all experience times of testing, which is normal for every human being. But God will be faithful to you. He will screen and filter the severity, nature, and timing of every test or trial you face so that you can bear it. Each test is an opportunity to trust him more, for along with every trial God has provided for you a way of escape that will bring you out of it victoriously."* Whatever you're going through, those things are not unique or new. Other couples have worked through the issues and so can you. Recognizing that your problems are not unique, will give you hope. With humility, allow God to guide and help you through the issues. Holy Spirit is always there to encourage and facilitate the growth that He has planned for both of you!

3. "My spouse should know exactly what I need"

As much as we'd like to believe, your spouse cannot read your mind. You have to communicate for mutual understanding. Remember to communicate with love, as described in 1 Corinthians 13:7 *"Love is a safe place of shelter, for it never stops believing the best for others. Love never takes failure as defeat, for it never gives up."* Talk through your concerns and emotions and ask questions so that you can be understood. Clear communication will lead to more clear understanding for both of you. You'll be more in sync, where your needs will be recognized and more easily met.

4. "The kids always need to come first"

This is a real issue and one that could derail your relationship. Similar to being on a plane, as you hear the safety message before takeoff, "be sure to put on your oxygen mask and then help those around you". After your relationship with Jesus, the two of you need to focus on one another first. Matthew 19:6 is one reference of the power of oneness in a marriage. *"From then on, they are no longer two, but united as one. So what God unites let no one divide!"* Over time, division can take place without you knowing it. Nurture your relationship with each other as you prioritize the importance of your marriage. You'll be better prepared to assist and nurture your kids. As time goes on, you may not recognize each other when the kids leave the nest. If you don't put your spouse before the kids, your marriage could certainly suffer the consequences.

5. "I'm not in love with my spouse anymore"

Couples can get caught up in their emotions of love instead of the true biblical meaning of love, as found in 1 Corinthians 13. You will recall the verses and the significance as we've shared in chapter one. Love is described much more in action than in feelings. It's always wonderful to "feel" in love, but our actions, care and service to one another will ultimately produce significant emotions of love. If you think you've fallen out of love or if your relationship is suffering, recognize it as an opportunity to work on your relationship and deepen your covenant.

6. "Pornography doesn't hurt my marriage"

The statistics related to how many people are either addicted to or that frequently subject themselves to pornography is staggering. Stop believing that pornography isn't doing anything to your marriage. There are countless studies describing how it kills relationships and hurts couples. According to the book, "Fight the New Drug", "An increasing number of couples in therapy report that pornography is causing difficulties in their relationship." 1 Corinthians 6:18 *"This is why you must keep running away from sexual immorality. For every other sin a person commits is external to the body, but immorality involves sinning against your own body."* Research shows that pornography use is linked to less stability in relationships, increased risk of infidelity and greater likelihood of divorce. Eliminate pornography in your marriage.

7. "My spouse will change eventually"

We are all different and unique. We all come from different backgrounds with all kinds of experiences and baggage. Although your spouse might change their mind on little things, the bigger fundamental issues and the things they're most passionate about, they may not. Many times, the change that you want to see in the other person is really a change that is about to occur in you. Recall your dating memories and the long discussions about your future together. Embrace your differences and appreciate the fact that you can function as a couple while disagreeing on certain things. Ask Holy Spirit to guide you and lead you through the change that He has for you in your marriage!

8. **"My marriage and spouse are supposed to make me happy"**

Happiness and real joy comes from The Lord and your relationship with Him. Psalm 16:11 does a wonderful job of sharing this truth. *"Because of you, I know the path of life, as I taste the fullness of joy in your presence. At your right side I experience divine pleasures forevermore"*. The more we can tap into the biblical truths of life, the more confident we will be in the Joy of The Lord and our relationship with Him. Your spouse isn't supposed to satisfy all of your specific needs. Think about this...What if God intended marriage to make us holy more than happy? It's a great question that Gary Thomas asks in his book "Sacred Marriage". If you look to your spouse to make you happy and expect them to meet needs that were intended to be met by God, it will be frustrating and exhausting for both of you. Thoughts or the expectations for your spouse to always make you happy will only lead to unmet expectations and disappointment.

9. **"My marriage is past the point of repair"**

If you're not in a physically, mentally or emotionally abusive relationship, your marriage isn't past the point of repair. We have seen God do great work in many marriages. God can and does resurrect marriages where there is abuse, but it requires a different set of tools and an investment of time. Psalm 103:10 says *"You may discipline us for our many sins, but never as much as we really deserve. Nor do you get even with us for what we've done."* God is not holding back blessings or putting things together for "plan B". There may be consequences for things we've done, but we know that God is for us and will finish the "good work" He started in each one of us. Expect His best and share hope with each other. There are ways for you and your spouse to rekindle your love and rebuild the relationship you once had. Once you stop believing these lies about your marriage, it'll be much easier to love your spouse, give of yourselves and build a happy marriage. God has a deep desire for us to experience His blessings and join in the ideal marriage that He has created!

10. "My marriage shouldn't be this hard"

All marriages have their issues, no matter how perfect they look from the outside or on social media. The bigger issue is that few couples talk about them, so we assume that everything is good. Every marriage takes work. As you see and experience great marriages, you can be assured that they have worked incredibly hard, with diligence over many years. Paul was intentional when he wrote to the church of Corinth about marriage and relationships. 1 Corinthians 7:27-29 says *"If you are married, stay in the marriage. If you are single, don't rush into marriage. But if you do get married, you haven't sinned. It's just that I would want to spare you the problems you'll face with the extra challenges of being married. My friends, what I mean is this. The urgency of our times means that from now on, those who have wives should live as though without them."* Our gaze should be on Jesus and through that relationship with Him; through Him, we will be equipped and prepared for a significant relationship with our spouse. Experience the powerful vertical relationship with Him and Holy Spirit will lead you to a meaningful horizontal relationship with others!

Summary

The list of 10 items above is just an example of the lies we've heard over the years, working with and counseling couples. Each couple and each marriage is very different from the other. Everyone will deal with temptations and challenges differently. When you have negative feelings or thoughts about your marriage, take time to share those with each other and develop a discipline to nurture TRUTH. Remember to implement and apply the biblical truths you've learned and call on Holy Spirit to help you. Remind yourselves of your identity in Christ and listen to what God has to say about your marriage! Expect His best and receive all the blessings that He has to share with you!

Questions/Activities/Activations/

There is real significance for going through the questions in each chapter. No matter how you're going through this material, the conversation and the transparency that comes from open discussion with each other will CHANGE your marriage.

Question One: Of the list above, which lie or lies do you struggle with and why? What actions can you take to refute those lies and stand strong in God's truth?

Question Two: How can we make practical use of the biblical descriptions of truth found in Proverbs 6:23 and Colossians 4:6? How can we relate and apply what we read in God's Word?

Read Matthew 4: 1-11. Ask Holy Spirit to guide and reveal to you the challenges in responding to the temptation of lies.

TAKE ACTION: Take a moment to recognize how far you've come in this process and appreciate one another for the change that is taking place in your lives. Even small steps of progress can offer hope and anticipation for what's next. Talk about the changes you've seen in each other and affirm your commitment to your marriage and to one another.

Notes and Ideas:

Chapter 11: Expectations

"Setting appropriate expectations"

All of us at one time or another have experienced a moment at work, in a social setting of some type, or have been engaged in conversations around expectations. They can be very memorable and very impactful. The person communicating the key message says, "I expect you to do this, or I expect you to do that"? As this message is being delivered, what is the purpose of this type of direct communication and how is it heard by the listener? It's expressed directly because someone is really trying to set a strong expectation with the message of *I expect*.

Think about how this fits into your relationship as a couple. When do we use the wording, *I expect* when we share a message with each other? Expectations are thoughts and attitudes about how I think things should be or could be. Whether you're aware of it or not, we all have expectations for every aspect of our lives. All of them have been uniquely formed and established from our own unique past experiences. When expectations go unmet, it can be extremely frustrating. You and your spouse will have different expectations in a number of areas of your lives which could create tension in your relationship. When expectations go unmet they are often the beginning of conflict. The way you deal with and respond to unmet expectations will have a direct effect on how you experience oneness in your marriage.

One of the easiest ways to bring attention to this powerful aspect of your marriage is to visit expectations every day. Setting meaningful expectations in your relationship can be as easy as asking questions about what each of you can expect from the day ahead. Knowing what to expect allows each one of us to understand and appreciate what's next, what could or should happen TODAY. It provides a foundation of what I can count on, or what I can rely on. This may sound too simple, but over the years we have heard stories from couples who haven't established any kind of expectation with one another. Having the thought of, "she knows what I expect", or "he understands why I feel this way", can be recognition of misunderstanding and a need for more conversation.

Biblical Truth: Proverbs 13:12, Psalm 62:2, Philippians 4:8, Proverbs 22:3, 1 Corinthians 13:7, Psalm 73:25

UNMET expectations and their effects

Think about the expectations that you have throughout your day and in your relationship with each other. You have expectations for when you go to sleep and when you wake up. You have expectations for who will perform different daily tasks, who will be responsible for cooking, cleaning and taking out the trash. As you work through these items, even without knowing it you're sending signals for expectations by default. "He takes out the trash because that is what the man does". "She does the cooking because that's what my mom did when I was growing up". What if that's not the case or what if that wasn't a part of my upbringing? Expectations for even the simplest of tasks need to be discussed. The items listed above may be easy, but what about talking through where you plan on spending holidays, how you're going to raise the kids or how available are you going to be for sexual intimacy? The list continues to grow and you need to set appropriate expectations. You need to clearly communicate with them before they become unmet and a source of frustration and conflict.

A verse that may be helpful in this area is Proverbs 13:12. *"When hope's dream seems to drag on and on, the delay can be depressing. But when at last your dream comes true, life's sweetness will satisfy your soul"*. Dreams, thoughts, ideas and expectations are all kept in our own minds, but until you share them openly with our spouse they will be misunderstood or unmet. Be sure to discuss these openly before the unknown or unmet expectations escalate and you hold these against your spouse. Having the thought that your spouse hasn't paid attention, or they haven't heard or don't understand, will only make things worse. This misunderstanding could lead to bitterness and you'll begin to think negatively, allowing anger to grow when it could have been easily avoided.

Taking steps for successful expectations

Donald Baucom, a psychology professor at the University of North Carolina, studied marital expectations for a decade. He found that people get what they expect. People with low expectations tend to be in relationships where they are treated poorly. People with high expectations tend to be in relationships where they are treated well. This suggests that by having high standards and higher expectations, you are far more likely to achieve the kind of relationship you want, rather than looking the other way and letting things slide. Having appropriate expectations and sharing them with your spouse are key ingredients for a successful life together.

The steps below can be as easy or as lengthy as you choose. These are YOUR expectations of each other. There is no right or wrong way of doing this. The key is to have a healthy and meaningful conversation with each other.

Talk through your expectations together

This may sound a little too obvious, but awareness is the first step to many things that lead to change, including the identification of your own expectations. Ask Holy Spirit to prepare the way for a meaningful conversation together. Recognizing the source of your own expectations will lead to a healthy conversation with your spouse about what you expect in your relationship. Expectations come from many sources, including things around you today. They come from family, friends, church, social media, movies, books and many more. You're not typically aware of your own expectations until they go unmet. The real significant step in this conversation is defining the source and determining whether or not the expectation you have in your mind is reasonable.

Discuss them ahead of time

Think of the times when you have had the biggest challenges or disappointments with unmet expectations in your relationship. This may raise your level of awareness of how simple the solution can be. Be intentional and set aside some time to talk about your expectations together. Remember, your ideas and thoughts about the upcoming weekend are clear in your mind, but they need to be communicated clearly and understood in your spouse's mind. Again, this might sound overly simplified but the power of communicating the specifics of what you're thinking and allowing your spouse to hear you, can be a very big deal. Never assume.

Think the best of each other

Thinking the best of each other is a key discipline in life. Establishing this as your first thought can make a significant impact in many life situations with your spouse and with others. Thinking the best allows you to see your spouse as God sees them. For those times when your expectations aren't being met you're not thinking negatively or feeling that your spouse is doing this intentionally. It sounds like giving your spouse the benefit of the doubt and offering grace and kindness that comes from Holy Spirit. "Don't take the bait" comes to mind again, as we recognize how evil wants to steal, kill and destroy. Your flesh may want to do one thing, but the power of Holy Spirit that is working in you, wants the best for you and your marriage.

Ask Jesus for His help

When there is challenge, frustration or fear, call on the name of Jesus to assist you. Our power comes from Him. When we try to deal with earthly things that are controlled by emotion and other outside sources, it's time to call on Him. He will guide you and provide direction. Your spouse may disappoint you; He never will. It's a great reminder that God is the only one that will provide all of your needs. With that in mind, you may have placed your spouse on a pedestal and set unreasonable expectations of them that they cannot meet. This will create disappointment and frustration for both of you. Allow God's love to work in and through you, as you offer grace to your spouse. Psalm 62:2 says, *"He alone is my safe place; his wraparound presence always protects me. For he is my champion defender; there's no risk of failure with God. So why would I let worry paralyze me, even when troubles multiply around me."*

Great Expectations

Even as you're reading this you may be thinking about your own situation and how your spouse is feeling. You have thoughts and expectations in your own mind right now, just as they do. They may be thinking about their own unmet expectations and frustrations. Take time to recognize and appreciate your own independent thoughts and ask your spouse about their expectations now, after reading through this chapter. This is a great opportunity for both of you to participate in a significant conversation with each other. Please understand and appreciate that both of you are the source of your unmet expectations with each other. Taking responsibility for how you handle your emotions through this exercise can be a great way to honor God throughout your life together.

Questions/Activities/Activations

This chapter on expectations and wisdom is one of the most significant in the book. The content and ideas shared here are meaningful, but they are just the beginning of the journey. Take time to work together and learn more about setting those "great expectations" with each other. As you go through the questions below, take time to really understand and apply the information that you've read.

Question One: Share the source of your own expectations for marriage. How were they formed?

Question Two: As you identify the different expectations you have for each other, what are the biggest challenges you face?

Question Three: How do you react when you have unmet expectations? How can you honor God and your spouse the next time this happens?

Activity: Take a moment to read Psalm 73:25, Proverbs 22:3, Philippians 4:8 and 1 Corinthians 13:7. Recognize how these biblical truths relate to the "steps for successful expectations" and describe how they relate to these steps.

Talk through your expectations together

Discuss ahead of time

Think the best of each other

Ask Jesus for His help

Solutions/ Suggested resources: Dr. Gottman and his team at the Gottman Institute continue to provide meaningful information and studies on many of these topics. Please reference additional information at www.gottman.com

*Be intentional about your communication with one another. The power of sharing your thoughts and ideas, as it relates specifically to your expectations will bring life and a better understanding into your relationship.

*Recognize the cultural differences that may exist between the two of you. We have experienced great revelation in this area and suggest that you appreciate how cultural differences affect your level of communication with one another.

*Continue to pray and ask Holy Spirit to lead you into the powerful marriage He has planned for you.

Chapter 12: Mutual Respect

At this point in the book you may have recognized that your level of awareness and your connection with one another has changed and changed for the good. You are more aware of who you are and how God has made you, uniquely and different from your spouse. Your understanding of your differences may actually bring challenges in your marriage to make you stronger as a couple. As you go through the material and discuss the questions throughout, we have seen miraculous change in couples as they've gone through the chapters on communication and expectations. We have also seen significant change in couples through these last few chapters. They become the building blocks for intimacy and the launching pad for a new and refreshed life together. The key outcome to all of this information is to bring you closer to Jesus. Your investment of time is to deepen your relationship with Him and ultimately with each other. In this chapter you will experience additional solid biblical truth in the following verses.

Biblical Truth: Psalm 139:13-14, Ecclesiastes 4:9-12, Genesis 1:27-28, 1 Peter 3:7, Philippians 2:3-4, Genesis 2:24, Ephesians 5: 33

Our differences bring strength

It may be hard to remember, but there WAS a first time that you and your spouse met. Think back for a moment and recall the emotions and the setting of your first meeting. Do you remember what got your attention and brought the two of you together? What were the attractions? How did you meet for the first time? First meetings are full of specific impressions, but in that first meeting were you aware of how different you were? Of course not, you were attracted to each other through a number of independent emotional points of interest. What were those points of attraction? Replay the moments in your mind and as you do, recognize where you are today as you review those specific memories. Do you recognize and understand how your *differences* could have brought you together? The understanding of your differences will guide you in knowing how to celebrate your spouse and assist them in becoming all that God has planned for them.

There is and will only be ONE you. God has created each one of us as unique and different individuals, to bring honor to Him and to each other. Those differences go beyond just male and female. You are different in your physical appearance, your personality, your talents and gifts, your background and your life experiences. Those differences and unique qualities are the things that brought you together as a couple. Those qualities were attractive and charming at some point, but now they may be irritating and frustrating, depending upon the time and situation. Your awareness and understanding of your differences is a powerful step to oneness in your marriage.

Utilizing your differences for The Kingdom

Take notice and recognize how God can use your differences as complements and appreciate how the two of you can do more together than apart. Psalm 139:13-14 *You formed my innermost being, shaping my delicate inside and my intricate outside, and wove them all together in my mother's womb. I thank you, God, for making me so mysteriously complex! Everything you do is marvelously breathtaking. It simply amazes me to think about it! How thoroughly you know me, Lord.* As you read these verses take comfort and be reminded of who you are and how God made you. He made you for a relationship with Him and with each other. Our unique differences are God given, from our Creator and have been placed in us intentionally. There is greater power and a stronger bond with each other because of our differences.

Another very different aspect of our lives is the list of gifts that we have been given, as seen in 1 Corinthians 12. Spiritual Gifts are not only unique, but they are shared in the body of Christ FOR the body, as we serve together in unity. Please read chapter 12 and chapter 14, as the list of gifts is described and explained. Our ability to recognize how we fit together in the body, as well as with each other will open new doors to acceptance and understanding that may not have existed before. Again, this is all about our differences and how we work together to serve The Kingdom. Ecclesiastes 4:9-12 provides a powerful reminder of who we are together, as *"two are better off than one, for they can help each other succeed."*

We recognize our differences, now what?

As you read through the material and respond to the questions above, you may be recognizing your own differences. You may even be thinking about how those differences bother you. Even now your mind is directing you to those thoughts of your differences and how they have either challenged you or brought joy into your relationship. No matter what you're thinking and no matter what you've experienced in the past, God has directed us to live with our spouse in an honorable way. 1 Peter 3:7 states it this way. *"Husbands, you in turn must treat your wives with tenderness, viewing them as feminine partners who deserve to be honored, for they are co-heirs with you of the "divine grace of life," so that nothing will hinder your prayers."* These verses are directed to the husband, but the underlying principle should be applied to both husbands and wives, as we live our lives together. There is real power in what is being communicated, as Peter is recognizing a couple being co-heirs and divinely connected with each other, spiritually intimate with Father God. We are to live with each other, honoring the relationship in an understanding way, so as not to hinder our prayers. We are directly connected with each other through Holy Spirit.

Study, honor and celebrate your differences.

As we live with each other, in all of our differences, we are to study and celebrate those differences. What does it look like to honor and study your spouse? Whether it's been one year or many years in your relationship, there are a number of things that you have studied in your spouse, even without you knowing it. What characteristics do you admire about your spouse? The list may be long or it might take you some time to come up with anything. As you study your spouse, you honor them with your thoughts and your appreciation for who they are and how God made them. Take a moment and see them as God sees them. Recognize what happens with your own thoughts and emotions. Understanding brings empathy and awareness for who they really are according to what God has planned for their life.

You can be an encouraging partner and support the work that He is doing in each of you. Having an understanding of their preferences, their gifts and unique abilities, will allow you to better serve them by putting their needs first. Philippians 2:3-4 states, *"Be free from pride-filled opinions, for they will only harm your cherished unity. Don't allow self-promotion to hide in your hearts, but in authentic humility put others first and view others as more important than yourselves. Abandon every display of selfishness. Possess a greater concern for what matters to others instead of your own interests."* Your lives together are a training ground and a life-long preparation for eternity. Enjoy the process of getting to know one another and recognize the significance of how the relationship may be changing you. Getting to know your spouse is an unselfish way of looking outward and will take time and attention. It will take intentional effort as you ask questions, talk and listen, purposely pursuing one another. The results of your efforts will build and grow your relationship into something special for the two of you to enjoy and for others to see.

As you begin this process and take those first steps in studying your spouse, ask yourself some questions about your spouse. Do you know how to pray for your spouse? Do you know their hopes and dreams? Do you know what brings them joy or what brings them frustration? What keeps them up at night or what challenges do they face during the day with work, kids or other issues? When you live intentionally with your spouse, studying them and putting them first, Holy Spirit can provide additional understanding and power for you to do much more than you could on your own.

Through the power of Holy Spirit that lives within you, YOU CAN...

*Serve your spouse in humility, putting their interests above your own.

*Have a greater concern for what matters most to your spouse.

*Celebrate their unique giftedness and personality.

*Enjoy all that God has provided you, as a helper, partner and mate.

Genesis 2:24 describes our lives together with our spouse as "one flesh". We are directed to live with each other in an understanding and honoring way, as we work toward oneness and support each other as co-heirs and Kingdom builders.

Questions/Activities/Activations

This chapter on honoring and studying your spouse can be powerful and life changing, as you take time to understand and appreciate your complements. Take time to go through the questions below and really understand and apply the information you've read through. Working through the questions will bring growth in each of you and encourage good conversation. Enjoy the process.

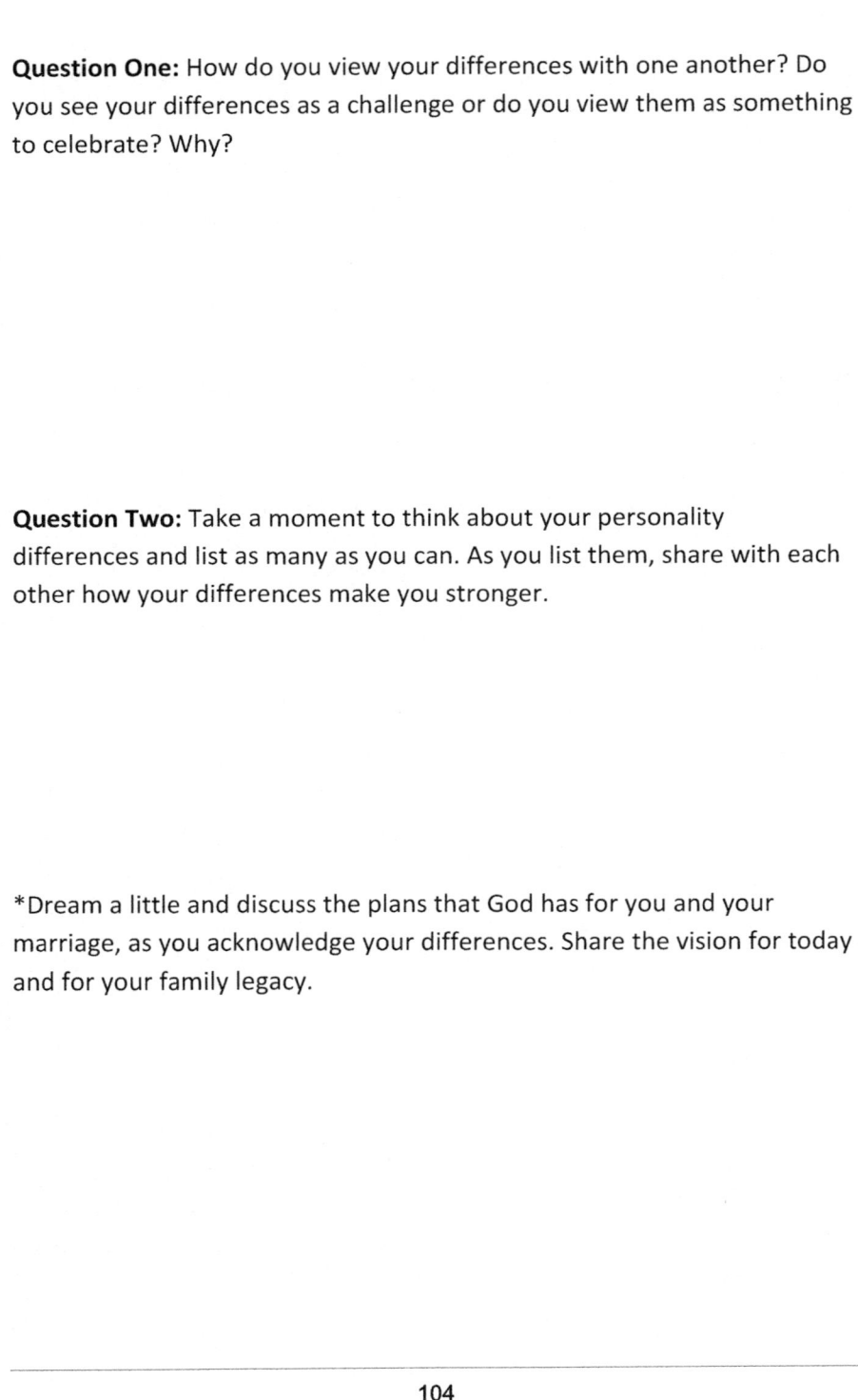

Question One: How do you view your differences with one another? Do you see your differences as a challenge or do you view them as something to celebrate? Why?

Question Two: Take a moment to think about your personality differences and list as many as you can. As you list them, share with each other how your differences make you stronger.

*Dream a little and discuss the plans that God has for you and your marriage, as you acknowledge your differences. Share the vision for today and for your family legacy.

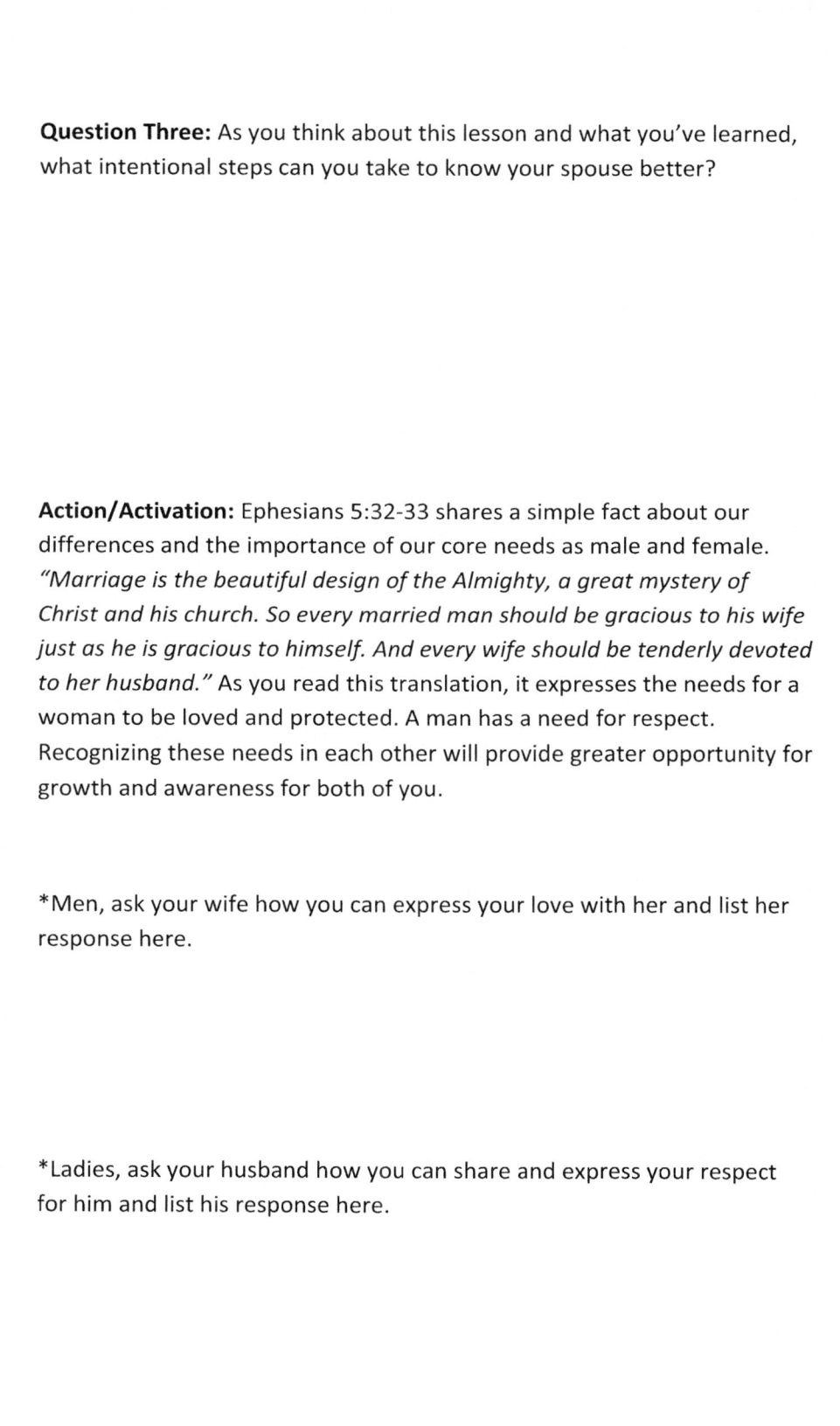

Question Three: As you think about this lesson and what you've learned, what intentional steps can you take to know your spouse better?

Action/Activation: Ephesians 5:32-33 shares a simple fact about our differences and the importance of our core needs as male and female. *"Marriage is the beautiful design of the Almighty, a great mystery of Christ and his church. So every married man should be gracious to his wife just as he is gracious to himself. And every wife should be tenderly devoted to her husband."* As you read this translation, it expresses the needs for a woman to be loved and protected. A man has a need for respect. Recognizing these needs in each other will provide greater opportunity for growth and awareness for both of you.

*Men, ask your wife how you can express your love with her and list her response here.

*Ladies, ask your husband how you can share and express your respect for him and list his response here.

Celebrate your spouse's differences on a regular basis and recognize how God has created each of you differently. How has God brought you and your differences together for His Kingdom work? There is real power in what the TWO of you can accomplish, serving together and serving one another. List as many of them here as you can!

Please consider taking a spiritual gift assessment of some type. There are many to choose from. The investment will lead you in identifying your own giftedness, which will bring power to your marriage.

Chapter 13: Intimacy

Each one of us experiences a typical day with a wide swing of emotions, experiences and encounters. At some point over the course of our lives, many of us come to realize that we don't control very much. Becoming aware of that fact and responding accordingly, we come to know that we can control our actions and our attitudes, that's about it. Our actions and attitudes take place and happen in an instant, right now in the present. To be fully present we need to be open and available to what's happening around us right now, not in the past, not in the future, right now. To be fully known and to be fully present we need to focus on what's happening in front of us, at the moment. I've heard it described as being in the middle of the "already and the not yet". **Intimacy**, emotional intimacy, happens in the middle of our already and not yet. Sharing in that emotional intimacy with one another is the act of being present with your spouse. It is one of the most important things you can offer your spouse each day. Being present has been proven to be one of the most important positive attributes of a couple's emotional health, which leads to an awareness of recognizing each other's emotional responses. It is the simple act of being emotionally available; placing yourself in the conversation, listening and being attentive to what is taking place in the now. This kind of understanding will lead to advances in other areas of your life together as well. We'll read about that in the next chapter, but please recognize the significance of this in your own life and appreciate what happens.

As we experience more and more of life, we may recognize the significance of letting go and allowing Holy Spirit to offer His comfort and His presence. Allowing Him to lead and prompt our next steps can be a far better way to live. Jesus wrote His love letter to us in the book of John chapters 13-17, describing how life would be for His disciples, preparing them for life without His physical presence. There can be a real benefit to release control and allow Holy Spirit to lead us. He will encourage us and

He will guide us into a more intimate relationship with Him and with others, just by asking. The more we let go and allow God to work in and through us, the less self-focused we become. Establishing a relationship with Holy Spirit will lead to a more intimate relationship with Him and with your spouse.

Daily application of intimacy

As Christians we have been given the mind of Christ. He lives in each one of us that have accepted Him as our Lord and Savior. How much more powerful could the relationships with our spouse be, if we knew how to tap into that God given power? 1 Corinthians 2:15-16 states, *"Those who live in the Spirit are able to carefully evaluate all things, and they are subject to the scrutiny of no one but God. For who has ever intimately known the mind of the Lord Yahweh well enough to become his counselor? Christ has, and we possess Christ's perceptions"*. We know that the Triune God can be a challenging thing to comprehend, but recognize that He has provided all that we need, to live life well and conquer those things that seem out of reach. Matthew 7:7-8 is a great reminder for all of us. *"Ask, and the gift is yours. Seek, and you'll discover. Knock and the door will be opened for you. For every persistent one will get what he asks for. Every persistent seeker will discover what he longs for. And everyone who knocks persistently will one day find an open door"*

Practical steps toward intimacy

Providing biblical references and the inclusion of Holy Spirit is a great first step, but many ask us about the practical, day to day process. How do I make good use of the information and move forward in the intimacy that He has for me? Knowing self is a critical step. Having the interest and desire for more will drive you to action. When I know myself and recognize the need for freedom in Christ will pave the way for Him to facilitate your growth in intimacy. Barriers to intimacy include 4 areas that need to be addressed and "cleansed" from your life. The subject of inner healing and deliverance has filled many books, so this simple introduction is just that, it's an introduction. Please be mindful of these areas and seek guidance in your community. There is a growing network of resources that can provide help and assistance in the areas of fear, hatred, the occult and sexual sin. Each of these four areas include specific areas that can be addressed and dealt with, so we can all live in the freedom that Christ died for!

Intimacy defined...

"To fully know and be fully known by others" is a pretty good definition of intimacy. Being known is one of those things we hear about as we're seeking personal growth or when we're in a healthy small group trying to get to know one another. Opening up and allowing your spouse to know *you* may be more difficult than *you* getting to know them, as we read in the last chapter. It is one of those areas where we all seem to have difficulty, allowing others to see who we are beyond the façade, beyond the walls we've built. We *know* who we are, and we *know* our thoughts and failings, let's just keep it that way right? Opening up and allowing the walls to fall might be challenging for many of us. Recognizing our own failings and sharing openly with others about those failings is a big step, but it's one worth taking and can lead to great change. It's not until we expose our flaws and show the real self with others that we experience real freedom. Freedom comes from our own step of faith, to share and to be open and reveal who we really are with others. Proverbs 27:17 states *"It takes a grinding wheel to sharpen a blade and so one person sharpens the character of another."* Sharpening takes place when we share with one another. It happens when we trust and open up. Real change and personal intimacy takes place in being vulnerable. Unfortunately in the world we live in, when we express vulnerability it is recognized as being weak. That couldn't be further from the truth. The ability to share your "real self" with people you trust can be instrumental for your own personal growth. Sharing in a vulnerable way, without worry of being rejected or ridiculed, is a position of power. It is the first big step to freedom. The spiritual intimacy that follows will lead you to the real change that God has planned for all of us.

Biblical Truth

Please know and recognize that God loves you and He already knows your thoughts. We read in Psalm 139:2 *"You perceive every movement of my heart and soul and you understand my every thought before it even enters my mind."* Why do we think that we're hiding something? We are already fully known by Him aren't we?

Romans 5:8 says, *"But Christ proved God's passionate love for us by dying in our place while we were still lost and ungodly!"* When we become known, loved and accepted by our spouse, even with all our past failures, we will have a more tangible understanding of His kind of love. Marriage is a wonderful training ground for all of us. It is God's earthly example and preparation of the marriage of Christ and His church, His bride.

Psalm 103 shares a wonderful message of God's love for all of us and His deep desire for our lives. It is about praising Him and all that He has provided. It reminds us of how we are to respond to His love, as we love others. **Read Psalm 103** and make use of these words and other passages, as you continue to search yourself and ask for Holy Spirit to guide you through the process. You are not alone; He wants the best for you and has brought the two of you together to do just that.

Your investment in intimacy

Like any good investment, intimacy will take time and effort. It will require some intentionality on your part. It will require some thought, as the two of you review an idea to discuss and openly share. It may include the details about something that you have kept hidden and may not want to share, because of past hurts or disappointments. These feelings are often significant to you because of what you experienced growing up. We know that these experiences absolutely affect who you are. They have shaped and developed you into the person you are today. Your relationship with your spouse is evolving every day, one way or the other. The more you share the details of your life, the better you will know each other and respond with sensitivity and understanding. There is a wonderful reciprocal relationship that is available for you. With time and effort your investment will lead to the fruitful and productive life that God has planned for both of you!

Return on your investment

One of the most powerful benefits of being known by someone else is that they may help you with your blind spots, or those areas that you may not be seeing.

*You may have issues in your life that you haven't recognized or you're not aware of. A loving spouse can assist in making you aware.

*A good marriage relationship will help you in working through things you haven't recognized on your own.

*Intimacy builds the bond of love and trust together with your spouse, will bring change and personal growth that you've never experienced.

*We are all being refined and a subtle revealing is taking place that will lead to even greater growth and maturity.

The payoff and the result of your openness will lead to more intimate conversations, more personal awareness and a deeper appreciation for how much God loves you. He is preparing and equipping you for eternity WITH your spouse's help.

Ongoing benefits and relational dividends

If you were asked, "What are your spouse's hopes and dreams"? What would you say? Is that a conversation that the two of you have had to even know the answer? Real intimacy involves being open and honest with your spouse, about everything. As you work through the long list of items to discuss and share, recognize how or why it might be difficult to share honestly. What are you feeling and why? The ability to trust and not feel judged is a big step into openness and vulnerability that you might find uncomfortable at first. Keep stretching yourself and keep building the trust that leads to honest, open conversation.

Your ability to be intimate and share openly with others can be a powerful step into the freedom that Jesus has for you. The evil one wants you to think otherwise. He wants you to avoid the truth and the transparency that comes with intimacy. He wants you to deny that any of the bad stuff happened in your life for fear that you will share it, deal with it and step out into freedom. Denial is rooted in fear, while confession is rooted in hope. You are a powerful person with the ability to make your own decisions for a life full of passion and love, as God intended. He wants to share Himself through you to others. Having a deeper level of intimacy requires transparency and a vulnerability that isn't typically experienced in our daily lives. This is what makes intimacy so unique, different and special.

Love and acceptance

We live in a world that is full of judgement and opinions, likes and performance based responses. We are recognized and rewarded by our good deeds and corrected or rejected by our bad deeds. God loves us no matter our situation or position, as we read in Psalm 103:10-11 *"You may discipline us for our many sins, but never as much as we really deserve. Nor do you get even with us for what we've done. Higher than the highest heavens—that's how high your tender mercy extends! Greater than the grandeur of heaven above is the greatness of your loyal love, towering over all who fear you and bow down before you!* Romans 2:4 offers a beautiful reminder of God's love and acceptance of each one of us. *"Do the riches of his extraordinary kindness make you take him for granted and despise him? Haven't you experienced how kind and understanding he has been to you? Don't mistake his tolerance for acceptance. Do you realize that all the wealth of his extravagant kindness is meant to melt your heart and lead you into repentance?"* You are loved by God and He wants the very best for you. His desire is for you to repent and turn back to Him. He has brought you together with your spouse to assist in the process of bringing you into a closer relationship with Him and with each other.

Questions/Activities/Activations

You've just invested time in your marriage related to intimacy, one of the most powerful sources for a strong and meaningful relationship. As you think through the questions in this chapter, take time to recognize where you stand in your own intimacy. Anticipate the benefit to come, from talking through the particulars of where you are in the process of knowing each other.

Question One: While reading the chapter, what was the prominent emotion you were feeling about intimacy and what was shared? What is Holy Spirit sharing with you about your intimacy with Him and with each other?

Question Two: Take a moment to think about your own hopes and dreams for the future. Dreams or failures, which are more difficult to share? Why?

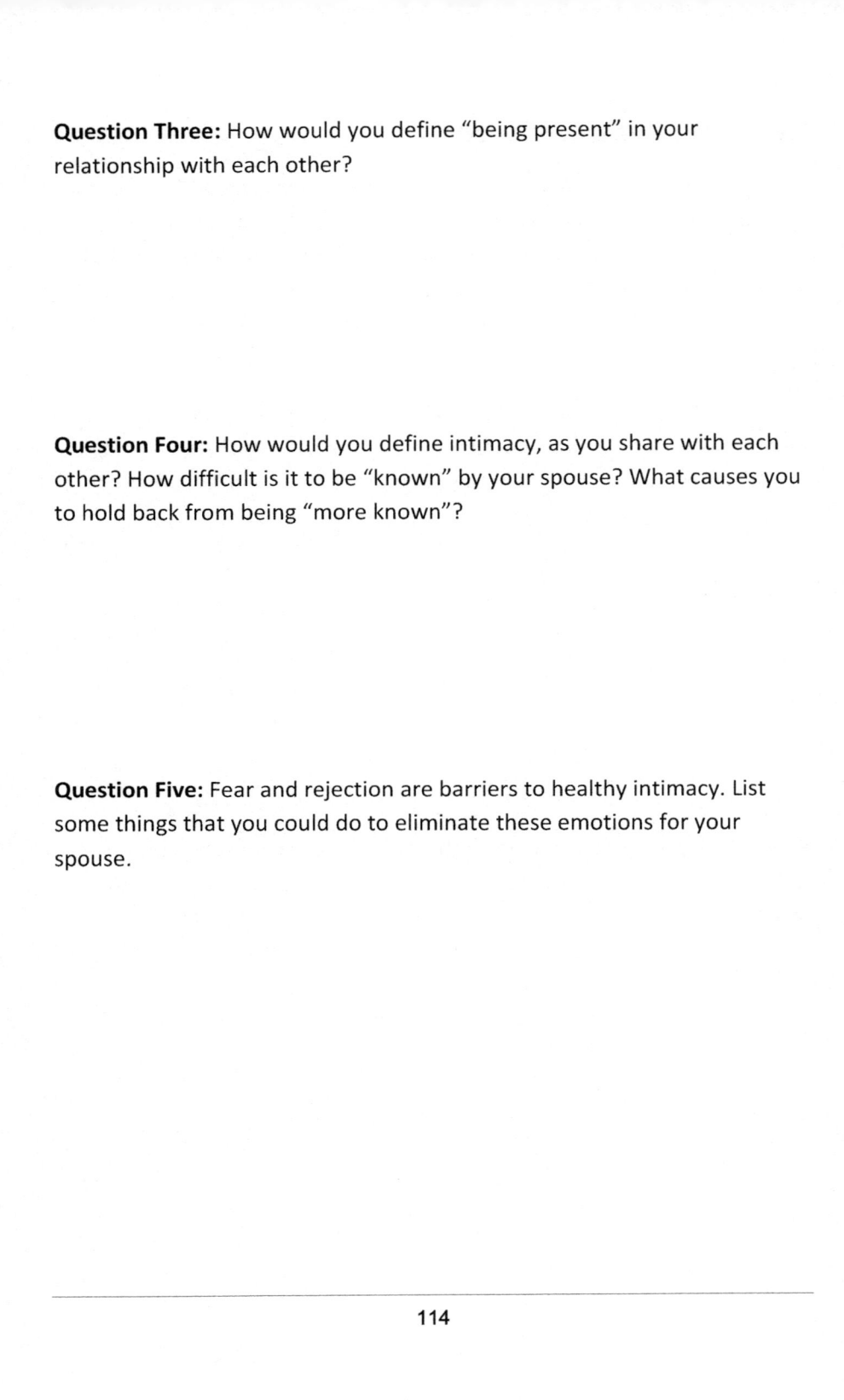

Question Three: How would you define "being present" in your relationship with each other?

Question Four: How would you define intimacy, as you share with each other? How difficult is it to be "known" by your spouse? What causes you to hold back from being "more known"?

Question Five: Fear and rejection are barriers to healthy intimacy. List some things that you could do to eliminate these emotions for your spouse.

Activation: Ask each other about expectations for the day and the week ahead. Intimacy is all about getting to know each other. Asking questions is one of the best ways to open the discussion that leads to intimacy. Once you begin this practice during your morning routine, you'll appreciate how this becomes natural and deepens your relationship.

Final thoughts:

Being intentional about the above items will build something special for both of you. Listening and being available to each other, knowing that you're being heard, are great building blocks to intimacy. Listening isn't about having all the answers, its acknowledging each other and becoming a safe place for conversation. Always be committed to growing together. As you put forth the effort, being vulnerable, understanding and intentional, the two of you will create a connection and a unique bond. You have expressed an understanding that you're both committed to the same thing, feeling equally yoked, seen, known and loved.

Notes and Ideas:

Chapter 14: Physical Intimacy

As we build a mutual understanding with one another, we create a deeper appreciation for our differences and the characteristics that drew us together as a couple. It takes time, diligence and intentionality as we've shared. The intimacy that you establish, to truly know one another fully without worry or concern, will lead to a deeper physical intimacy as well. The way you think and the emotions that you bring into a relationship are real. Recognize that the most important organ for physical intimacy is the brain. The brain is a protector and director of our thoughts. Success comes when we are free from those mental roadblocks of the doubts and concerns that take us elsewhere. When we allow ourselves to be vulnerable and share with each other openly, we experience the freedom that Jesus died for. Galatians 5:1 says, *"At last we have freedom, for Christ has set us free! We must always cherish this truth and firmly refuse to go back into the bondage of our past"*. The sacrifice of Jesus is complete, for ALL aspects of our lives. Our trust in Him and all that He has planned for us will continue to lead us into a life of abundance. His immeasurable love and the outpouring of His blessings call us to be thankful and dependent upon Him each and every day. We need to trust Him with our lives. Without trust and the many things we've discussed in previous chapters, intimacy will be stunted or immature. The more you trust in Him and trust in each other, the more intimacy and physical connection you will have together.

Biblical Truth: Galatians 5:1, Genesis 1:27-28, 31, 1 Corinthians 10:31, Matthew 5:28, 1 Corinthians 13:5, Philippians 2:3-4, Romans 14:15, 1 Corinthians 7:3-5, Proverbs 5, Song of Songs 7:9-11

Daily application:

Let's talk about sex

Sex is a powerful source of intimacy. It has the power to join and the power to pull apart. It can bring beautiful oneness for a married couple, or it can divide and separate. Sex is the joining of two people, establishing a covenant relationship with each other. In our culture today, sex has been misplaced, diluted and minimized in its importance. We need to recognize and appreciate the true meaning and purpose of sex in our lives. Sex is the physical reminder of the covenant relationship that God has made with us. With a true appreciation and understanding, it can be a wonderful and powerful part of any marriage. Much of this depends on your own opinions of sex and how it has influenced you.

We all have our own opinions and past experiences around the topic of sex. Those experiences and influences have created all types of unique and different responses in our minds. Whatever the case or however it's been shaped in your mind; it is a subject that needs to be addressed. The goal of this chapter is to move you closer to oneness as a couple. This will happen through open conversation and an appreciation for the fact that Holy Spirit is always with you and never leaves the room. With that in mind and with that understanding and awareness, ask Him to join you in a deeper appreciation for what He has planned for you.

Too little or too much?

Male and female, we can become overwhelmed with the cultural challenges of sex in our society. It is used in advertising, movies, media and in just about every aspect of our daily lives. Sex sells and it has been influencing all of us from the very beginning of time. Even as you're reading this you may be thinking about how you've been influenced in your own opinions about the subject of sex. Your view of sex and the influence it has had on you throughout your life will lead you to either minimize or maximize sex. The purpose of this chapter is to help you better understand that sex is a wonderful gift from God and it is to be enjoyed by both man and wife, in a covenant relationship, throughout your married life together.

Too little

If you tend to think about sex as a chore, that it's wrong or something that needs to be done out of obligation, you may be minimizing the role of sex in your marriage. Your understanding and point of view may have been formed through your own guilt or shame from your past. It could be because of how you were raised, what you were taught, or if you experience pain during intercourse. In some cases, your opinion has been formed from past abuse of some kind. Through our work over the years we've recognized that there is a high percentage of abuse that has taken place, sometimes without knowing or remembering the event. This topic is a highly sensitive one and needs to be recognized for additional counseling or professional help. Having some level of mutual awareness for past abuse can lead to significant conversations, which can lead to emotional healing for both of you. Additionally, sex should not be used as a negotiating tool used to manipulate or exert control in the relationship. No matter the situation, open conversation and honest discussions can lead to a much more emotionally healthy sex life.

Too much

If you tend to think about sex often, wishing you had more in terms of frequency or quality, you may be thinking too much of sex. If you think that your marriage would be better if you had sex more often, you may have an obsession with sex. You may be placing too much emphasis on sex which can lead to unmet expectations and pressures on your spouse. If you become angry without sex or you have emotional highs and lows depending upon the frequency of sex, you will both benefit from having an open and honest conversation together. Either way, whatever you're experiencing, the purpose of sex is intended to be an important part of a marriage, just not the MOST important. It is designed and meant for a married couple to enjoy and to deepen the intimacy that God has intended for you.

Sexual Challenges

We know from numerous studies and years of data, that both men and women have been negatively affected by pornography. We shared a few thoughts about this in a previous chapter, but it's worth mentioning again. Knowing the statistics and the significant impact that pornography is having on individuals, couples and marriages today will allow you to discuss this subject openly and ultimately deal with the issue. Pornography has become available to anyone with a phone and has been more accepted because of its availability. We have become conditioned to its normality and because of that; it has overcome and overwhelmed too many marriages today. On one of the world's largest pornography website, well over 90 billion videos are viewed daily by more than 64 million visitors, 26 percent of them female. This chapter is not meant to stir up controversy, it's meant to stir up conversation and awareness in both of you, to be diligent in protecting what is yours.

Be aware of and watch for these indications that pornography may be causing a problem:

- A person's sex life becomes less satisfying.

- Pornography causes relationship issues or makes a person feel less satisfied with their partner.

- A person engages in risky behavior to view pornography, such as doing so at work.

- They ignore other responsibilities to view pornography.

- They view progressively more extreme pornography to get the same release that less extreme porn once offered.

- They feel frustrated or ashamed after viewing porn but continue to do so.

- They want to stop using pornography but feel unable to do so.

- They spend large sums of money on pornography, possibly at the expense of daily or family necessities.

- They use pornography to cope with sadness, anxiety, insomnia, or other mental health issues.

Know full well, the enemy is an enemy of marriage and he is here to kill, steal and destroy. It is our responsibility to lead and love others through their individual challenges. You may have an opportunity to step up in your own relationship and lead other couples that are dealing with similar issues. The power of Holy Spirit is on our side and He is fighting for us. It is time that we fight WITH Him and take back the sanctity and significance of sexual intimacy in our marriages.

What does a healthy, biblical sex life look like?

If your model for a healthy sex life has been formed by what you've seen on TV, movies or the culture around us, you may have more questions. What does the bible tell us about sex and appropriate boundaries for what a healthy Christian sex life looks like? There are a number of specific biblical answers for us today, just as there were in the early church. The Apostle Paul had a number of responses to those precise questions found in the information below.

Sex is selfless: 1 Corinthians 13:5, Paul mentions that *"Love does not traffic in shame and disrespect, nor selfishly seek its own honor. Love is not easily irritated or quick to take offense"*. Appreciate the power of these words, as you think about your own spouse and your relationship with each other. You are to view your spouse as more important than yourself. As you do, there can be wonderful reciprocation.

Sex is transparent: Paul shares in Philippians 2:3-4 *"Be free from pride-filled opinions, for they will only harm your cherished unity. Don't allow self-promotion to hide in your hearts, but in authentic humility put others first and view others as more important than yourselves. Abandon every display of selfishness. Possess a greater concern for what matters to others instead of your own interests"*. Establish a relationship built on trust where both of you can express your desires openly. Avoid demanding or focusing on yourself in this subject, just as you should in other aspects of your relationship. One of the most powerful ways to grow in your intimacy is to put your spouse first.

Sex is honoring and pure: Paul writes in Romans: 14:15 *"If your brother or sister is offended because you insist on eating what you want, it is no longer love that rules your conduct. Why would you wound someone for whom the Messiah gave his life, just so you can eat what you want?"* This is a statement about anything that would be offensive to another believer, especially your spouse. We know the significance of this statement with alcohol or other "unclean" items that could potentially offend another believer, but it also applies to this subject with your spouse as well.

Sex is exclusive: Matthew references additional thoughts on the subject, sharing Jesus comments on sex in chapter 5 verse 28. *"However, I say to you, if you look with lust in your eyes at a woman who is not your wife, you've already committed adultery in your heart."* This statement is all inclusive, as we look at anyone who is not our spouse. We live in a world of self-gratification and experimentation with so many different things and ideas. If you have had premarital sex or sex outside a covenant marriage you have created unhealthy soul ties that need to be broken. Please read 1 Corinthians 6: 15-18 for a complete understanding of the significance of this subject. Sex within a marriage is sacred and honoring and needs to be protected. To have any other thoughts, actions or activities beyond what is honoring, can be offensive and harmful to your relationship.

Biblical view of sex

There is no mystery as to how we lost our way in marriage and that the divorce rate is what it is. The enemy has a target on marriage, because IT IS the foundation of our communities, our churches and our families. For years, we as Christians have looked the other way and allowed an improper view of sex to creep into our lives and into our communities. This in turn has diluted the sanctity of sex and therefore directly affected our marriages, families and our culture. Biblical truth and the proper view of sex need to be expressed and discussed in the church and in each one of our marriages.

Sex is a gift from God

God shares His directive and confirmation of sex in Genesis 1:28 *"and God blessed them in his love saying: Reproduce and be fruitful! Populate the earth and subdue it."* And again in Genesis 2:24 *"For this reason, a man leaves his father and mother and becomes unselfishly attached to his wife."* They became one flesh as a new family"

If the purpose and goal of sex is primarily for pleasure, then other people are just objects to be used for sensual gratification. The Christian perspective is that the purpose of sex is relational, with pleasure as the by-product, not the focus. The Bible teaches that sex bonds two souls together. It is so powerful that it is only safe within a committed, covenant marriage relationship. God knew what He was doing when He limited sex to within a marriage. Sex was created by God for joining us together for intimacy and for our enjoyment. If you don't believe that to be true you may find it difficult to give yourself away completely to your spouse.

You are God's creation

Genesis 1:27 *"So God created man and women and shaped them with His image inside them. In His own beautiful image He created His masterpiece. Yes, male and female, He created them."*

Believing that your body is good and that God created man and woman in His image will lead you to better understand His identity in YOU. Today's culture puts so much pressure on physical appearances that many of us don't like our body, which can hinder thoughts of intimacy. If you see your body as a gift from God, rather than something to be ashamed of, this belief can lead you to improved intimacy with your spouse.

Sex is to be enjoyed

Proverbs 5:18-19 *"Your sex life will be blessed as you take joy and pleasure in the wife of your youth. Let her breasts be your satisfaction, and let her embrace intoxicate you at all times. Be continually delighted and ravished with her love!"* 1 Corinthians 7:4 *"A husband has the responsibility of meeting the sexual needs of his wife, and likewise a wife to her husband. Neither the husband nor the wife have exclusive rights to their own bodies, but those rights are to be surrendered to the other."*

Sex wasn't designed or given to us for just "being fruitful"; it was given to us to be completely and fully enjoyed by both husband and wife. Embrace sex as a gift from God and you will better appreciate the inclusion of Him in the process, through Holy Spirit. Sex that is described in the Bible is first and foremost about intimate friendship. It is about cleaving to your God-given other, becoming "one flesh". Sex is pursuing physical, emotional and sexual union. It is about submission, exploration, discovery, and delight.

Proverbs chapter 5 is a study in itself, in addition to the two verses above. Please recognize the significance and the warning that comes from King Solomon, as he is providing instruction to his son about avoiding promiscuity and reserving sex for marriage. He states that your wife is the fountain and the source to be drinking from, no one else. The entire chapter is wonderful instruction for all of us, as we read in verse 21. *"For God sees everything you do and his eyes are wide open, as he observes every single habit you have."*

God wants us to have a healthy sex life. Continue reading the entire chapter and ask Holy Spirit how He can better equip you for a pleasure filled life together, spiritually, emotionally and physically.

Sex is a powerful way to glorify God

1 Corinthians 10:31 reminds us of the significance of what we do to acknowledge Him in our lives. *"Whether you eat or drink, live your life in a way that glorifies and honors God"*.

Our ability to recognize and welcome Holy Spirit into every aspect of our lives will enhance everything we do. He wants us to include Him. It's a beautiful reciprocal relationship which includes the way we experience sex. We honor God in how we love, serve, show kindness and compassion for others and put our spouse first in the relationship. How you respond to the topic of sex can be a good indicator of your own spiritual growth and maturity. We pray for growth in every area of your lives.

With every relationship there will be a different experience or opinion with the subject of sex. Recognizing the significance of sex in your marriage will lead you into a more intimate, committed relationship with one another. You will have the rest of your lives to discover and explore your intimacy and how God has blessed you, as you continue to include Him in your marriage.

Final thoughts and reminders for the chapter

We appreciate the thought and reminder that "all of marriage is foreplay". Think about it as you go about your day. You may have an interest of engaging in sex tonight, but how is that making itself known throughout the day with your spouse? If you incorporate the idea of sex through your day, making comments and suggestions, you're on your way to establishing appropriate expectations. By brushing up against each other or sharing in some kind of tender moments, you are promoting the interest in the physical act of sex throughout your day. Those moments are yours to share, so establish them with your spouse as you choose. Have fun and switch things up, formulate and establish those times with each other throughout your marriage. Make every day an opportunity to connect and share your love, as you anticipate your sexual connection. Your thoughtful anticipation can be the biggest stimulant for both of you, as seen in Song of Songs chapter 7:9-11, *"For your kisses of love are exhilarating, more than any delight I've known before. Your kisses of love awaken even the lips of sleeping ones. Now I know that I am for my beloved and all his desires are fulfilled in me. Come away, my lover. Come with me to the faraway fields. We will run away together to the forgotten places and show them redeeming love".*

As we shared biblical truth and biblical references on sex, most of you may be surprised that there are specific biblical references to read, as we question the subject of sex in marriage. Studying and reading the words are one thing, sharing and discussing them with your spouse is quite another. If you desire a true and satisfying sex life with your spouse you will need to share in the conversation, you need to use your words. Being gracious and kind in this area will lead to great success and enjoyment for years to come. Remember the power of sharing expectations, as we shared in the previous chapter. You cannot just think or assume that your spouse knows what you're thinking or what your desires are without communicating. Be open and continue to earn the trust of each other and enjoy the process. Sex is a powerful God given gift to both of you. Make good use of the gift. Open it up, talk about it and share in open discussion about every aspect of it. A great sex life throughout your lifetime together doesn't just happen. It will take prayer, understanding and humility.

Questions/Activities/Activations

Question One: What questions come to mind about your own sex life, after reading this chapter? This is between the two of you. Ask Holy Spirit to lead you through an intimate conversation about this most significant subject.

Question Two: Of the FOUR verses on the biblical view of sex, what do you struggle with most and WHY?

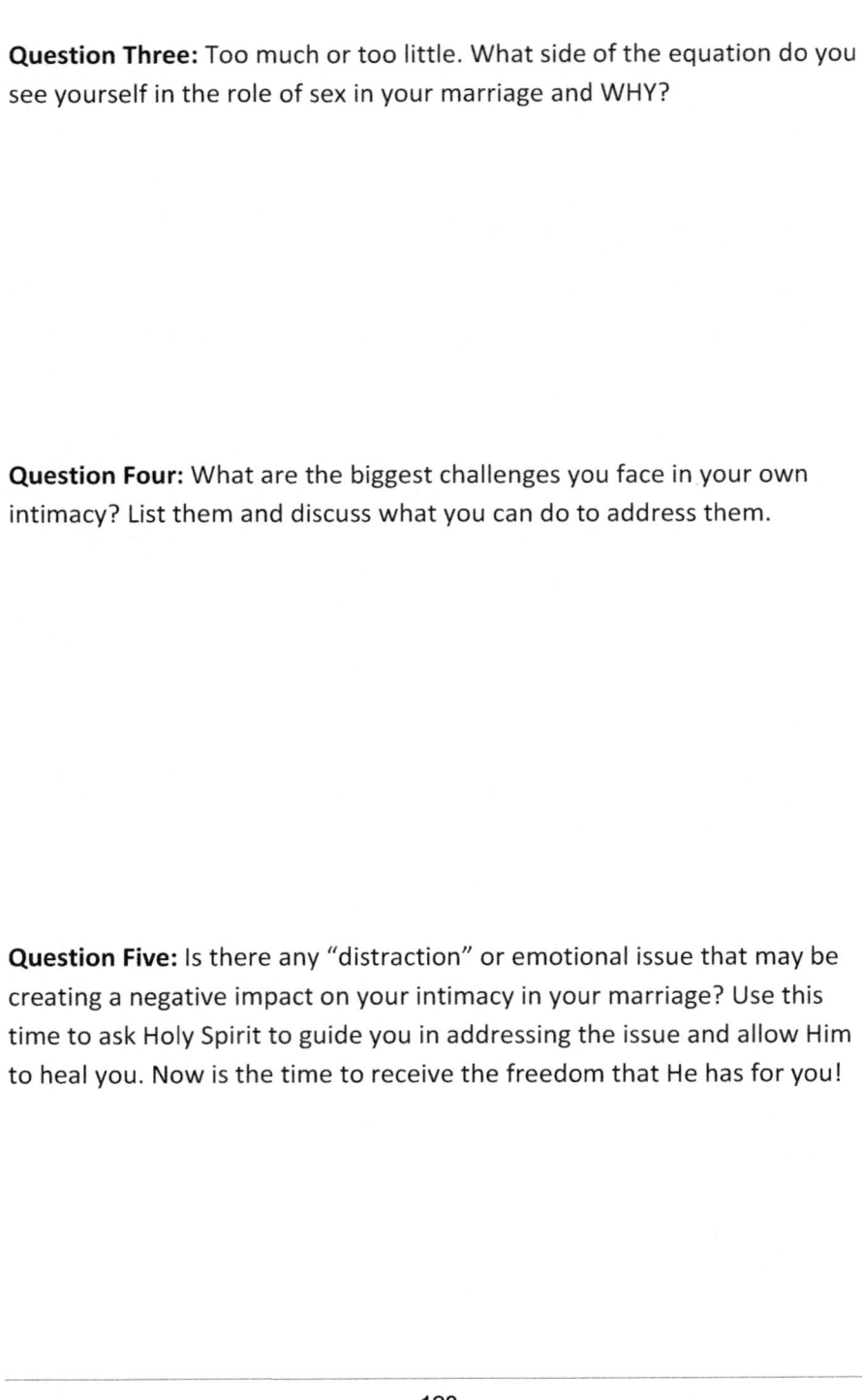

Question Three: Too much or too little. What side of the equation do you see yourself in the role of sex in your marriage and WHY?

Question Four: What are the biggest challenges you face in your own intimacy? List them and discuss what you can do to address them.

Question Five: Is there any "distraction" or emotional issue that may be creating a negative impact on your intimacy in your marriage? Use this time to ask Holy Spirit to guide you in addressing the issue and allow Him to heal you. Now is the time to receive the freedom that He has for you!

Study together: Paul's instruction to the church of Corinth, 1 Corinthians 7:3-5 *"A husband has the responsibility of meeting the sexual needs of his wife, and likewise a wife to her husband. Neither the husband nor the wife have exclusive rights to their own bodies, but those rights are to be surrendered to the other. So don't continue to refuse your spouse those rights, except perhaps by mutual agreement for a specified time so that you can both be devoted to prayer. And then you should resume your physical pleasure so that the Adversary cannot take advantage of you because of the desires of your body.*

Ask Holy Spirit what these words mean to you and your marriage? Take time to pray and read through the significance of the words expressed in 1 Corinthians. Invest some quality time together and make good use of your conversation, as you experience meaningful growth in your marriage. What are you hearing?

MORE READING: Song of Songs offers such a great love story and description of who we are with Christ and with each other. Chapter 2 verse 16 provides a great reminder of our oneness with Him. *"My beloved is mine and I am his"*. All of us are made for intimacy with God. Upon that initial separation from Him in the garden, our deep desire for contentment, satisfaction and love are always unfulfilled. We long for His return and the intimacy with the one for whom we were made. The good news is that Jesus is the groom who brings a new Garden of Eden when he returns.

Thought provoking quote...

"Satan encourages us to express something other than love through our sexuality; lust, selfishness, disobedience or lies. When these are the spirit behind sex, it is Satan who is glorified and not God."

From the book, "**When two become one**" by Christopher and Rachel McCluskey

Notes and Ideas:

Chapter 15: Oneness

"Marriage and Life-Long-Love"

When you read the word oneness, you won't recognize the word in your daily vocabulary and it's not typically used in everyday conversations. It doesn't come up because it's not a descriptive word that we tend to use. There is something very significant about the **oneness** that happens when two people come together spiritually, as well as physically. You know it when you see it and especially in your own experience. Have you ever stopped to observe couples out and about during your day? Couples that have been together for a long time share in a oneness that is noticeable. They move together, they seem to dance through life in a beautiful cadence that the Lord has orchestrated, blessed and ordained. This kind of oneness and partnership doesn't just happen; it takes work and is blessed by Father God. Significant and meaningful relationships take place through prayer, awareness and diligence. They happen through years of conversation and sacrificial love. They prosper through an understanding of the covenant relationship they engage in and are committed to. This level of work and commitment ultimately leads to a level of intimacy and trust that each one of us can experience and enjoy.

Marriage is different and more unique than any other relationship we enter into. It was recognized in the garden too, as stated in Genesis 2:18 *"It is not good for the man to be alone. Therefore, I will fashion a suitable partner to be his help and strength."* God had a plan for us to be together, to share and to be an encouragement to one another. In Ephesians there is specific instruction for how a man is to encourage his wife, in acknowledgment of the sacrifice of Jesus. Ephesians 5: 25-28 states *"And to the husbands, you are to demonstrate love for your wives with the same tender devotion that Christ demonstrated to us, his bride. For he died for us, sacrificing himself to make us holy and pure, cleansing us through the showering of the pure water of the Word of God. All that he does in us is designed to make us a mature church for his pleasure, until we become a source of praise to him—glorious and radiant, beautiful and holy, without fault or flaw. Husbands have the obligation of loving and caring for their wives the same way they love and care for their own bodies, for to love your wife is to love your own self."* The power behind these verses should remind all of us of the significance of our marriage relationship. Your spouse is uniquely positioned in your life to assist, encourage and love you in ways to promote your own spiritual growth, just as God had planned.

Paul continues to share great wisdom, through Holy Spirit in the book of Romans 8: 29, on the significance of our spouse and their influence in our spiritual lives. *"For he knew all about us before we were born and he destined us from the beginning to share the likeness of his Son. This means the Son is the oldest among a vast family of brothers and sisters who will become just like him."* As Christians, our purpose and our focus is to become more like Jesus. He has uniquely provided our spouse, our helpmate and partner for the abundant life that He has planned in advance for each of us.

Biblical Truth: Genesis 2:18, Ephesians 5:25-28, Romans 8:29, 1 Thessalonians 5:14, Hebrews 10:24, 1 Thessalonians 4:10, John 5:15, James 4:1-3, Hebrews 10:25, 2 Corinthians 1:3-4, Matthew 6:19-21, Proverbs 22:6, Mark 10:45, 1 Corinthians 7:28, 1 John 13:34-35, 1 Peter 5:6-11, Philippians 2:1-2

Daily application:

Great power and instruction in the Word

Read through these verses in 1 Thessalonians below and **Experience a FULL LIFE of encouragement throughout your life and in your marriage.** 1 Thessalonians 5:14-22 *"We appeal to you, dear brothers and sisters, to instruct those who are not in their place of battle. Be skilled at gently encouraging those who feel themselves inadequate. Be faithful to stand* *your ground. Help the weak to stand again. Be quick to demonstrate patience with everyone. Resist revenge, and make sure that no one pays back evil in place of evil but always pursue doing what is beautiful to one another and to all the unbelievers. Let joy be your continual feast. Make your life a prayer. And in the midst of everything be always giving thanks, for this is God's perfect plan for you in Christ Jesus. Never restrain or put out the fire of the Holy Spirit. And don't be one who scorns prophecies, but be faithful to examine them by putting them to the test, and afterward hold tightly to what has proven to be right. Avoid every appearance of evil."* It is difficult to fully address these beautiful verses in the depth they require here, but please take a moment to appreciate the power of these words for your own life in this simple way.

Instruct those that are not in their place... The Greek translation refers to those "not being in battle formation", but being disorderly or out of place. Recognize that avoiding the issue or allowing the issue to continue isn't love. One of the most significant roles of a spouse is to assist in sharing loving admonishment and the truth with each other. Offering this type of guidance in a loving, caring way will promote personal growth in each of you.

Be skilled at encouraging... The words that are shared here are from Holy Spirit through the Apostle Paul. Visualize him sharing these instructions with his audience. He is expressing the need to encourage each other in a skillful way, by and through The Spirit, with care and compassion. Sharing encouraging words with each other when you're feeling inadequate or when you need to add caring attention can be one of the most significant things you offer to your spouse.

Be faithful to stand your ground... As Christians we deal with a lot of daily challenges. As we stand, we stand firm in our Faith and in the strength of Holy Spirit. We carry His supernatural strength in us, against all that life throws at us. Helping each other stand firm means to stand with each other together, holding each other up as one flesh, as one powerful team against the enemy.

Demonstrate patience... As we serve together, change will happen in each of us over time. Through love, truth and intentional prayer, patience will be rewarded.

Resist revenge... Some days will require more prayer than others, but always resist the first reaction as seeking revenge. Humility, grace and the ability to forgive will be the greatest tools for you to use, as you resist taking the bait of the evil one. Your ability to respond in love and with meaningful conversation, will lead to a much better outcome.

Let joy be your feast and make your life a prayer... Who doesn't enjoy these words prescribed for each one of us? "I will feast on joy and make my life a prayer" for myself, my spouse and those around me. Make this a consistent practice and think of how your lives would be. This will certainly create an attitude of gratitude and thanksgiving. We give thanks for all that God has done for us through His son Jesus Christ.

Never restrain the Holy Spirit... As we acknowledge Holy Spirit as ONE in the Trinity, we must recognize His power and direction in our lives, as stated in John 14:17. *"And I will ask the Father and he will give you another Savior, The Holy Spirit of Truth, who will be to you a friend just like me—and he will never leave you. The world won't receive him because they can't see him or know him. But you know him intimately because he remains with you and will live inside you."*

Welcome prophetic words and put them to the test... The two of you have been ordained and established for the good work of Father God. Listen for His word and the prophetic words He has through other believers. Test them and hold onto the truth that is being shared with you, as you love and lead each other and those that you serve.

Avoid every appearance of evil... This may seem obvious but sometimes we miss what evil looks like. Even the appearance of evil can change and adapt in our everyday lives. We may become conditioned to a familiar spirit that slowly makes its way into our lives and into our marriage.

A life-long love together

This final chapter and the lessons in it are just the beginning. Now you can make good use of the tools and conversations that we've had throughout the study. Your level of awareness has increased and you have recognized a few new things in each other. Sharing openly with each other will continue to serve you well. You will develop a deeper level of trust and realize that your spouse is on your side, you're on the same team working together. As you live a full and meaningful life together, you'll recognize that you're on a live stage with each other 24/7, exposing yourself and your marriage like never before. It may make you feel uncomfortable, but please appreciate that with exposure comes growth and a closer relationship with Jesus. Your spouse is your companion and friend; they have a front row seat to your life and the life you will live together. Think of them as a witness to all that God has planned for you. You have been given the privilege to assist them in bringing the change that Holy Spirit has for both of you.

Diligence and intentionality

At this point you've experienced change. You have shared in the power of grace, forgiveness and recognized the unique intimacy that God has introduced you to. Now it's time to take what you've learned and plan for the future. Make good use of the tools and pursue a life of continuous growth and maturity in your faith and with each other. We all need encouragement as we go through our life's journey, so always keep that in mind as you continue to support and encourage one another. Paul was a great encourager throughout the new church, no matter what his circumstance. He is a great example for us to follow.

Philippians 2:1-2 *"Look at how much encouragement you've found in your relationship with the Anointed One! You are filled to overflowing with his comforting love. You have experienced a deepening friendship with the Holy Spirit and have felt his tender affection and mercy. So I'm asking you, my friends, that you be joined together in perfect unity—with one heart, one passion, and united in one love. Walk together with one harmonious purpose and you will fill my heart with unbounded joy."*

1 Thessalonians 4:10 *"Indeed, your love is what you're known for throughout Macedonia. We urge you, beloved ones, to let this unselfish love increase and flow through you more and more."*

Colossians 3:14-15 *"For love is supreme and must flow through each of these virtues. Love becomes the mark of true maturity. Let your heart be always guided by the peace of the Anointed One, who called you to peace as part of his one body. And always be thankful."*

Growing in your faith and strengthening your marriage takes an investment of time and energy. It takes some planning and forethought as you go about your day. How you do this is completely up to you, but recognize that this is just the beginning. This study and the conversations you've had are meant to stir up your Spirit. They are meant to get you moving to develop yourselves into advocates and ambassadors for our faith and for marriage, in every place you go and in every position you hold. With Holy Spirit as your guide and friend, empowered with the words from Paul, what is your next step? We would suggest using this model shared by Paul to the church in Philippi. Philippians 4:8-9 *"Keep your thoughts continually fixed on all that is authentic and real, honorable and admirable, beautiful and respectful, pure and holy, merciful and kind. And fasten your thoughts on every glorious work of God, praising him always."* What a beautiful message of staying the course and being grounded in the power of our God, Jesus our Savior and Holy Spirit our companion and friend.

Focus on yourself and all that YOU control, not trying to change the other person, but praising God for all that He is doing in your own life. He will not only change you, but He will lead your spouse in this change process as well. You first, then the two of you together.

Open up and share who you are, with your spouse and with others. The enemy wants to shut you down and keep you separated from the love and encouragement of others. Isolation is one of his easiest and most effective tools for keeping you from your destiny. Hebrews 10:25 offers great encouragement for this subject. *"This is not the time to pull away and neglect meeting together, as some have formed the habit of doing. In fact, we should come together even more frequently, eager to encourage and urge each other onward as we anticipate that day dawning."*

Be an advocate for marriage with others. Your testimony and your marriage experience are uniquely yours. Be sure to express encouraging words with others from your own challenges, success and joys. Your testimony is powerful. 2 Corinthians 1:3-4 is another great reminder of biblical truth in this area. *"All praises belong to the God and Father of our Lord Jesus Christ. For he is the Father of tender mercy and the God of endless comfort. He always comes alongside us to comfort us in every suffering so that we can come alongside those who are in any painful trial. We can bring them this same comfort that God has poured out upon us."*

Stay diligent in all areas of your life. Life is full of activity and all kinds of change and excitement throughout our lives. Be aware of the distractions of this world, as you continue to mature and move forward in your life. Be diligent and aware of those distractions, daily. Stay focused on Jesus and ask Holy Spirit to cover you in all areas of your life each day. Make good use of the tools you've learned and incorporate them into your life and live them out. You are a powerful person with the ability to make informed decisions, as you make a difference in this world.

Serve, serve, serve. Mark 10:45 *"For even the Son of Man did not come expecting to be served by everyone, but to serve everyone, and to give his life as the ransom price for the salvation of many."* Now it's your turn to sow what you know into others. You play a significant role in eternity and can change the trajectory of a single person that will affect change in a couple, which will change a family for generations to come. What a blessing it is to serve with Holy Spirit guiding you. Others will see Jesus in both of you and in turn, they will want to know more about your story and your transformation.

Final thoughts...

There is such a need for positive, confident examples of Christ led marriages in today's world. After many years of serving wonderful couples, we were led to put these thoughts together. Holy Spirit is a real person and a real power in the Trinity. He continues to lead us, guide us and love us in a way that we've never been loved before. A relationship with our creator, through Holy Spirit can be so special and significant for your life as a believer. You will never be the same. We urge you brothers and sisters, in view of His mercy, to make a difference in our world. Make a difference in YOUR world, with those around you. Recognize how God designed you, how He blessed you and where He has placed you. You are right where you need to be, doing just what He has you to do. Pray and ask Holy Spirit what His plan is. Say yes and follow His prompting.

We are reminded of the simple direction and commandments that Jesus shared with us, as recorded by the Apostle John. The words in John 13:34-35 are familiar. *"So I give you now a new commandment: Love each other just as much as I have loved you. For when you demonstrate the same love I have for you by loving one another, everyone will know that you're my true followers."* "Everyone will know", gives me a reason to serve my spouse well. Others will see Jesus in me, sacrificially putting their needs first and purposefully setting them up for success. Celebrating your spouse and loving them significantly will bring even more attention to who you are in Christ; others will be clamoring for what you have and what you carry.

Take hold of each other and live a life of love, cherishing one another for the world to see. Step into your identity as man and wife, joined by Him, led by Holy Spirit to be an example of good works and powerful love for all.

As we close, one of our favorite blessings is found in 1 Peter 5:6-11

"If you bow low in God's awesome presence, he will eventually exalt you as you leave the timing in his hands. Pour out all your worries and stress upon him and leave them there, for he always tenderly cares for you. Be well balanced and always alert, because your enemy, the devil, roams around incessantly, like a roaring lion looking for its prey to devour. Take a decisive stand against him and resist his every attack with strong, vigorous faith. For you know that your believing brothers and sisters around the world are experiencing the same kinds of troubles you endure. And then, after your brief suffering, the God of all loving grace, who has called you to share in his eternal glory in Christ, will personally and powerfully restore you and make you stronger than ever. Yes, he will set you firmly in place and build you up. And he has all the power needed to do this —forever! Amen."

Questions/Activities/Activations

Some of the most significant change that takes place in couples is in the discussion of questions. Please be sure to review these questions, actions steps and activities as we wrap up and conclude with the final chapter and discussion. You've done a wonderful job of learning and sharing; now it's time to put all of that wonderful learning and experience to the test. It's time to live your lives together and show the world your very best.

Question One: As you've read through the chapters and grown in your relationship, what does "Oneness" mean to you? What does that look like for you and your marriage?

Question Two: How will the two of you be intentional about your relationship with each other going forward? How do you plan to utilize the experience, ideas and tools you've discovered here?

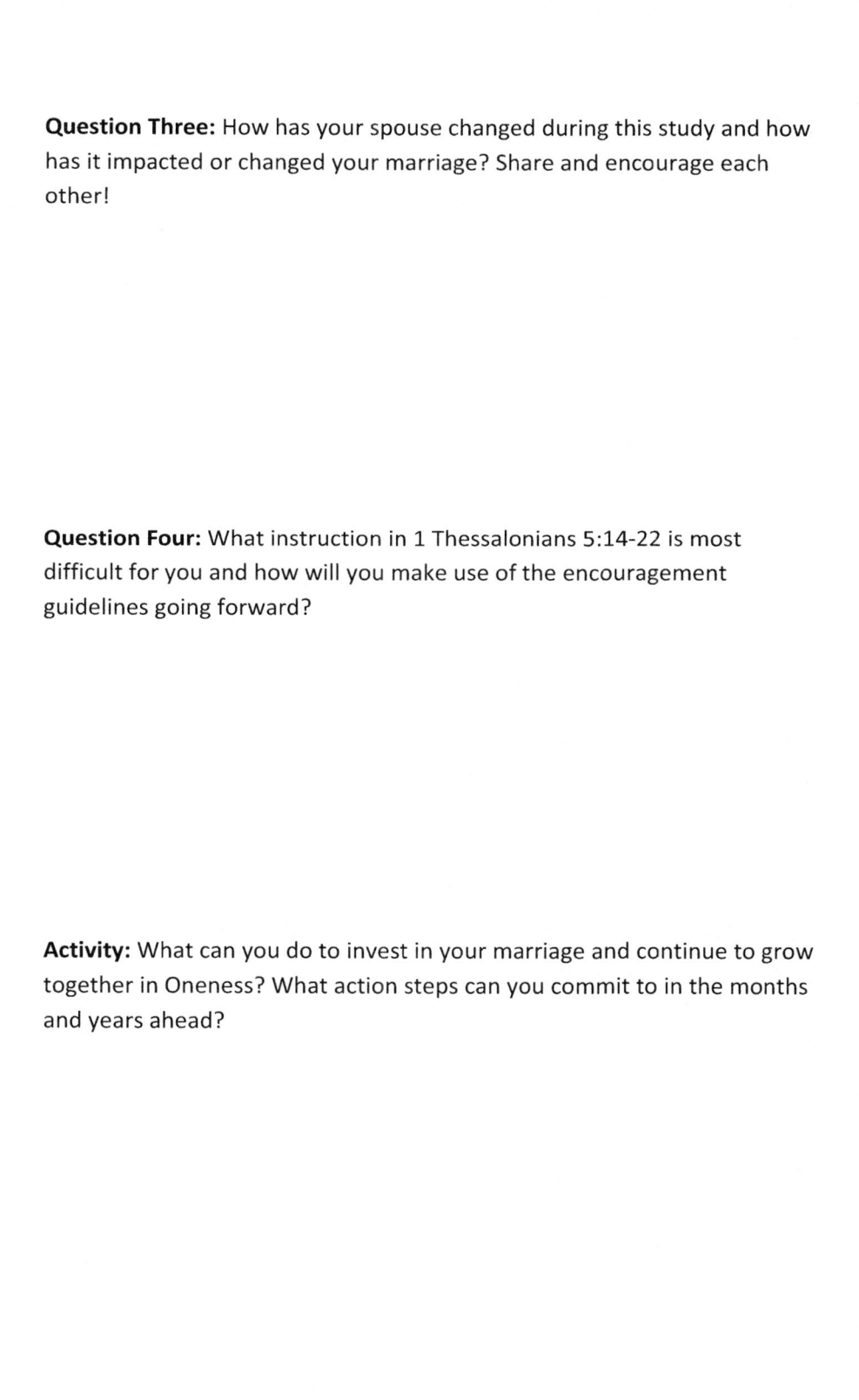

Question Three: How has your spouse changed during this study and how has it impacted or changed your marriage? Share and encourage each other!

Question Four: What instruction in 1 Thessalonians 5:14-22 is most difficult for you and how will you make use of the encouragement guidelines going forward?

Activity: What can you do to invest in your marriage and continue to grow together in Oneness? What action steps can you commit to in the months and years ahead?

Activation: Go back and look through your notes and highlight a few ideas or meaningful conversations that will lead to ongoing success in your marriage. Those significant items will be foundational to how you work together and hold each other accountable for what you've accomplished.

Go Forth and Represent!

Now is the time for change. Meaningful change, from each of you, that can make a difference in the world that we live in.

There is such a need for positive examples of what biblical marriage looks like and YOU can be that example.

You can be the example for many AND for many years to come! Go forth and be witnesses for the entire world to see!

Be thankful, be powerful and share all that you've experienced in your "SPIRIT FILLED MARRIAGE."

We would enjoy hearing from you, as you have testimonies and success stories to share. Email **info@spiritfilledmarriage.org**

Additional copies can be obtained for family, friends, neighbors or anyone who will benefit, through Amazon.com

Printed in Great Britain
by Amazon